MODERN
MENTORING

D1572634

Randy Emelo

PRESS

ATD Press is an internationally renowned source of insightful and practical information on talent development, workplace learning, and professional development.

ATD Press
1640 King Street
Alexandria, VA 22314 USA

Ordering information: Books published by ATD Press can be purchased by visit-
ing ATD's website at www.td.org/books or by calling 800.628.2783 or 703.683.8100.

Library of Congress Control Number: 2015933121
ISBN-10: 1-56286-933-7
ISBN-13: 978-1-56286-933-5
e-ISBN: 978-1-60728-498-7

ATD Press Editorial Staff
Director: Kristine Luecker
Manager: Christian Green
Community of Practice Manager, Human Capital: Ann Parker
Associate Editors: Melissa Jones and Ashley Slade
Cover Design: Bey Bello
Text Design: Marisa Fritz
Printed by Versa Press, Inc., East Peoria, IL, www.versapress.com

Contents

INTRODUCTION

Inception

This book has been gestating in my mind for the last 35 years. For me, mentoring is very personal and rooted in my career history. Had I not had the persistent guidance and influence of a network of more experienced practitioners throughout my career, I feel confident that I would have been doomed to a life of underachievement. Just like the Grateful Dead took their experiences of traveling on the road and turned them into the lyric, "What a long, strange trip it's been," I likewise have been on a long quest to create more effective learning relationships.

I enlisted in the U.S. Navy right out of high school and became a fabricator and welder, following my father's advice that I should learn a trade. My father was a machinist and my uncles worked in foundries or machine shops. My family was a living definition of the blue-collar worker. I had no idea what having a career meant; I was looking for a job. The navy helped me understand my unique capabilities and sent me to Nuclear Welding School, where I became certified to work on nuclear power plants. This event alone made me the most educated person in my family. I stayed in the navy for 10 years working exclusively on submarines. I have many wonderful and not so wonderful memories of my military service. I had no idea that I would eventually look back and recall all the important leadership and mentoring lessons that came from that time in my life. I'll share some of these stories in later chapters.

Toward the end of my last hitch in the navy, I began to realize my life's calling. As I looked back on my time in the military, I understood with certainty that I was more passionate about helping others develop than I was about fabrication or engineering. Leadership and leadership development became my all-consuming quest. I used my last two years in the navy to learn how to be a nonprofit leader and entrepreneur. I took a volunteer leadership position, which equated to a full-time nonpaying job, in a local organization focused on community development. I became immersed in small group leadership fundamentals.

Upon leaving the navy, I embarked on a six-year journey deep into nonprofit work. During those years I worked with and trained hundreds of leaders in North, Central, and South America. I earned my living in North America, and helped organize and lead medical relief and humanitarian aid trips to Central and South America. I also participated in three nonprofit startups. It was during this time in the nonprofit sector that the primary importance of mentoring began to grow clearer. Mentoring was very simple for me in those days. When I saw something in someone's life that I wanted to emulate, I would ask him to help me get it. I cannot remember anyone turning down my request and I took great pleasure in learning from the passion of others. Before I left the nonprofit world, I had the pleasure of leading more than 400 volunteer leaders who were, in turn, leading others. I doubt I will ever have the opportunity to learn as much about the transformational effects of mentorship as I did then.

During this time I designed and conducted dozens of leadership incubator groups that I dubbed turbo groups. These peer-driven collaborative learning groups would serve as a blueprint for my life's work. Today, I would call what happened in these emerging leadership groups modern mentoring. During the turbo group process, we would bring together a dozen emerging leaders and engage them in personalizing the principles of leadership behavior while leading community-based outreaches. We embraced learning-while-doing in a peer-to-peer, collaborative environment under the guidance of more experienced practitioners. There was a high degree of personal accountability in the form of sharing what was working and what was not. Creating these turbo groups had two immediate results: Those who were not serious about leadership dropped out quickly (about 35 percent), and those who stuck with the process emerged as confident leaders who made a difference.

My transition into working with for-profit organizations was not one that I would have predicted. In 1995, Tom Reed, a very close friend and mentor, approached me and asked if I would help him start up a training consultancy. The pitch that put me over the top and helped me commit to this new challenge went something like this, "Randy, people in these large for-profit organizations are struggling in isolation. They feel cut off and adrift in their careers. We have the opportunity to bring purposeful learning to them." Tom's words helped me understand the valuable service that we would be rendering to our clients.

So, I found myself co-founding Triple Creek (now River). For the first three to four years I learned how to create learning interventions for Global 1000 companies. I designed and delivered custom course content and curriculum, observational leadership assessments, performance management, and global learning processes.

This was during the rise of the e-learning revolution. We in the training profession were wrestling with the implications of the demise of the physical classroom. At Triple Creek, we had a burgeoning reputation as experiential trainers who relied solely on highly interactive course design and delivery. We licensed and supported hundreds of trainers who delivered our custom training. The thought of e-learning as a suitable replacement for our leadership courses was unfathomable. E-learning alone simply lacks context; and without context, course content is left to very limited perceptual understanding. So, when a major client asked me to design a course to help their midlevel leaders become better teachers, I immediately suggested that they allow me to create a scalable mentoring process instead. To my great surprise, they commissioned the project, and in 1999 Triple Creek created the first web-based mentoring software system. In 2000, we launched Open Mentoring (now River) as a commercially available e-mentoring software system.

During the last 14 years, I have had the pleasure of working with several hundred organizations as they sought to create more effective mentoring cultures. During that time, there have been many changes in the way that organizations view and apply mentoring. The message in this book represents the major lessons that I have learned during my career as I sought to help my clients create more productive learning environments.

My personal mission is to create a world of abundance and security through helping others to understand and practice modern mentoring. I hope you will join with me in making modern mentoring a more commonly used career development process.

1

Don't Put Mentoring in a Box

If you want to do more with mentoring, you've opened the right book. If you dream of broadening the impact that mentoring can have on your organization or about creating a culture in which learning from others is an embedded behavior, my hope is that you will find your answers on these pages.

That said, before we can embark on creating a modern mentoring culture, we must first take mentoring out of the metaphorical box where corporations have placed it, and instead begin to practice it in a vastly different way. To help explain why we must take mentoring in a new, more meaningful direction, let me tell you a story.

During the time I spent doing leadership development work in the nonprofit world, I read Robert Clinton and Paul Stanley's book, *Connecting: The Mentoring Relationships You Need to Be Successful* (1992). The larger message of this book ignited a passion in me that has inspired my life's work. Clinton and Stanley argue that mentors are all around us, and that mentoring has always been a broad practice. Anytime you learn something from others that can help your personal development, you are participating in mentoring.

Their book broadened the way I think about how people can influence one another from a learning perspective. They made me ponder whether mentoring is so wide-ranging that it includes historical mentors, such as Plato, Buddha, or Confucious, whose works have influenced entire cultures; and deceased mentors, such as Einstein, Darwin, and Steve Jobs, who still shape the way modern society thinks, acts, and works. I asked myself: Is my boss my only mentor? Could my contemporaries who live halfway across the world be my mentors? What about my peers with whom I practice, or the subordinates I manage and am constantly learning from—are they also my mentors?

For me, the answer to these questions is a resounding yes. People all around me have mentored me in one way or another. I decided that I would learn how to effectively implement and institutionalize this concept of mentoring that, to me, is a learning process that is inclusionary, networked, and centered on sharing knowledge with others.

With this in mind, I began to apply this idea of mentoring and use it as a relationship-centered developmental process for the people I worked with on nonprofit projects in Latin America. In an effort to help volunteers develop into leaders more quickly, I created "turbo" leadership development groups, where people would connect, share, and learn from one another. To my delight, these turbo groups not only worked; they worked far better than the process I had used before. My volunteers learned quickly and effectively in this networked manner.

With the help of my friend and partner, Tom Reed, I soon had one of those moments that could be described as an epiphany—where a once out-of-focus future became ever so clear. I would bring my concept of mentoring to for-profit organizations so that they could leverage it to achieve more effective learning. I thought to myself: *Imagine the power that unleashing this type of relationship-centered learning would have on the productivity and performance of an organization of 10,000, 20,000, or 100,000 people. What if organizations could start tapping into the collective knowledge of their workforce using this process? The results could be truly transformational.* As a result, I created the first e-mentoring technology and started on my quest to embed mentoring and broad social learning into the fabric of my clients' organizational cultures.

To my disillusionment, I discovered that while almost all organizations could see the benefits and agree with the broader concepts of mentoring as I saw it, the way they had traditionally been applying it in practice had made creating a new mentoring culture impossible. Mentoring took hold in the business world during the 1980s primarily as a way to advance diversity and inclusion efforts for women and minorities. There was (and still is) a lack of diversity in the upper levels of many organizations, and human resource departments attempted to address this issue by pairing up a female or minority employee with a hand-picked senior leader who could guide the protégé's development.

It was a laudable endeavor, but it affected an incredibly small number of people, typically around 1 percent of an organization. Corporations tried to address an enormous problem, which demanded more open social learning and knowledge sharing, with a very narrow and limited solution. Their efforts had unintended consequences—formalizing mentoring with rules and barriers to the point where it became exclusionary and extremely limited. In their application, corporations had unconsciously put mentoring in a box, and as a result put a lid on the benefits it could create.

Then as today, everyone in an organization could benefit from guidance from upper-level leaders (from people at all levels of the organization), but an organization's leaders most certainly do not have time to mentor every employee. Setting mentoring programs up so that there are only as many mentees as there are upper-level leaders to mentor them leads to social justice issues in which some employees receive special treatment and opportunities, while others are left out. This exclusionary practice is counter to the broader mentoring ideals that would benefit employees the most.

The traditional approach to mentoring perpetuates the idea that mentors are special and only certain people are qualified enough to share knowledge. The reality is no one person can have all the answers. Pinning all of your career aspirations and expectations on one person is ludicrous. Our world changes so rapidly and is so complex that I would wager there truly is no single person who could be your lifelong mentor, guiding you every step of your career.

This leads to another problem: Who is to say that the executive you would be paired with is the right one to guide you? What if you need to learn more about cross-channel partnerships or emerging technologies, but the executive assigned to you doesn't know about those things? Or what if your executive is the one who could use a mentor? How would that conversation sound?

In traditional mentoring, the task of matching people falls on program administrators. They act as gatekeepers who handpick participants and matches. Just imagine sitting in your office with a spreadsheet in front of you as you try to determine who gets matched. If you've ever run a formal program, chances are you don't have to try too hard to picture this outdated and burdensome process. The sheer amount of time it takes to simply select and match people makes it difficult to accommodate more than a handful of participants. Add to this the fact that many formal mentoring programs require administrators to guide the mentoring process and check in with participants, and you can see why these programs are so difficult to run effectively.

I've met many mentoring program administrators over the years, and it's fair to say they truly want what is best for their participants and are doing their best to make facilitating mentoring programs a meaningful endeavor. Unfortunately, they are going about it the wrong way. High-touch formal mentoring programs are time-consuming, costly, reach too few employees, and require too many resources.

Organizations are doing themselves more harm than good when they force connections between people. By requiring people to connect with one another in specific ways, organizations:

- limit who can talk, connect, share, and learn from one another
- stifle innovation and creativity
- perpetuate a mindset that treats adults like children
- build a reputation as a staid company, which can turn off prize candidates who decide to work somewhere else.

The bottom line is that we need to do away with the barriers that surround the current or traditional corporate practice of mentoring. We must force ourselves to ditch the spreadsheets, forget the limited populations we designate as being special enough to participate, and abolish the idea that any of us could broker relationships that have productive learning value for every single employee in our diverse workforces.

To release the transformative power of mentoring from the narrowly conceived box in which mentoring currently resides, leaders from all areas of an organization—business units, HR, talent, learning, and diversity—must embrace a new mindset about mentoring.

Combatting the Traditional Mentoring Mindset

Even though we know that mentoring has evolved well beyond its traditional beginnings, chances are that you will encounter people with a mindset that views mentoring as a formal, long-term, one-on-one, face-to-face practice in which an older mentor grooms a younger employee for a specific job. Those who feel strongly about the traditional practice of mentoring often question the expanded practice of modern mentoring. How many of these objections sound familiar?

- Leadership sees mentoring in a traditionalist fashion, and I can't do anything to change that. (And if my senior leadership doesn't participate in the process, no one will.)

- Modern mentoring (and the related social learning) will only appeal to people in younger generations, such as Millennials.

- We won't have enough mentors. If we open up the program, our small quantity of expert mentors will become inundated with requests.

- Traditional mentoring is how our organization has always facilitated learning, and none of our participants are complaining.

Don't let these opinions hold you hostage. Traditional mentoring mindsets will stifle any attempt at enabling a more open, relationship-centered way of learning. To break free from that mindset, embrace a more adaptive approach to mentoring in order to get modern mentoring programs off the ground at your organization. To learn more about combatting the traditional mindset, see Appendix I.

Here are four ways you can overcome these common objections and make modern mentoring thrive.

Figure 1-1. A New Mentoring Mindset

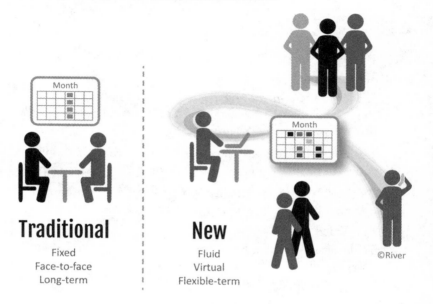

Traditional

Fixed
Face-to-face
Long-term

New

Fluid
Virtual
Flexible-term

©River

Change Your Terminology

Senior leadership will need to get behind your modern mentoring initiative in order for it to be successful. That said, many senior leaders likely participated in traditional mentoring during their careers and will tend to see mentoring in this way. Because of this, it may be difficult to change their mindset around mentoring. If you envision presenting modern mentoring to your senior leaders and having your ideas rejected, simply change your terminology. For example, you could refer to your initiative as social learning or learning collaboration.

Then, instead of having to split hairs over the definition of mentoring, you can focus on the substantial and scalable benefits of such a program. Most leaders can get behind any initiative that produces a smarter, more connected workforce that is better prepared to perform their jobs.

While on the topic, nonparticipation by senior leadership is *not* critically important for modern mentoring. Senior leaders are certainly key stakeholders who will need to support and champion the initiative, but the demographic with the most to gain from modern mentoring are those employees in the middle and bottom of the organization who still have a lot of room for personal and professional growth.

However, if senior leadership participation is non-negotiable for you, then you need to make participation easy for busy executives to fit into their workdays. I've found through my own experiences that executives will gladly participate if you make it clear it will not take too much of their time. As an executive myself, I feel the innate need to give back and recycle the knowledge that has helped me achieve my career success, but I don't have patience for time-consuming or difficult processes. I use my company's social learning technology, which makes participating in mentoring a quick five- to 10-minute process that I can easily fit in between meetings and projects. Time is today's ultimate scarcity. If you ensure that participation in your initiative is quick and easy, you'll find that your executives (and the rest of your employee population) will be more than happy to share their hard-gained knowledge and expertise.

Don't Fear Technology

Modern mentoring is scaled and enabled by technology, yet there is a misconception in the workforce that older employees can't or won't use new or social technologies. This is a fallacy; for example, a 2013 study by the Pew Research Center indicated that seniors were the fastest-growing group of social media adopters, with 45 percent of Americans over 65 using at least one social networking site. Social and digital technologies are the new normal for all adults, not just those who may have been early adopters or who are from younger generations. Additionally, all of today's employees work in the same fast-paced environment where most skills have a shelf life of 18 months or less. Regardless of age, workers want learning that matches their reality. They need ways to connect with peers to address knowledge needs in a more dynamic and fluid way. Modern mentoring helps remove barriers between people, adds context to training content, and allows knowledge to flow from person to person.

Look for Experts at All Levels

There once was a time when knowledge and information were scarce and the people who had access to them were few. Enter the Internet and egalitarian access to the digital world. Today's organizations are filled with knowledge workers and look nothing like companies of days past; knowledge and expertise is found throughout the entire organization (yes, even at the very bottom). This means that everyone can be an advisor in her area of expertise, which falls in line with modern mentoring's idea that everyone has something to teach and something to learn. If you encounter people who say modern mentoring programs that allow all employees to participate won't succeed because there won't be enough mentors, explain that learning from extreme experts does little to help a beginner. A beginner would learn best from someone with intermediate skills and knowledge. This saves the extreme experts for your intermediate learners, who will benefit from their advanced skills and knowledge. This broader approach opens up the scope of available advisors who will be able to support your inclusive and open modern mentoring environment.

Listen to What Is Not Being Said

A lack of complaints about your formal mentoring process does not equal complete happiness with it. It's no surprise that your formal mentoring participants (especially your mentees) aren't complaining about the process—it would be akin to career suicide if someone who is specially selected to receive exclusive treatment through formal mentoring complained about his inclusion in the process. And it's true that employees may enjoy and derive value from participation in a traditional program, but organizations that limit their social learning to formal mentoring only serve between 1 and 10 percent of the employee population. Not only does this cause social justice issues to arise in the minds of employees (both excluded and included), but it also limits the impact that relationship-based learning can bring to an organization. Beyond being fair, organizations have much to gain from scaling improved performance, engagement, and retention across their employee population by including everyone in modern mentoring. You can even wrap formal mentoring into your modern mentoring approach, which would allow you to offer the practice that serves the few, while also creating a way to serve the masses through a broader program.

Modern Mentoring for a Modern Workforce

Today's global complexity requires a nimble workforce that can adapt to rapid change, new demands, and unforeseen challenges. To succeed, companies must constantly innovate. Providing your organization's workforce with ways to connect, collaborate, learn from, and share with their colleagues across all levels, locations, and functions is critical—and it is the driving force behind modern mentoring.

The purpose of mentoring has moved away from getting a handful of people ready for leadership roles and shifted to a practice that focuses on three key areas:

- increasing an organization's intelligence (emotional, leadership, technical)
- enhancing an organization's ability to compete
- accelerating employee development.

This shift in purpose means that more people need to get involved in mentoring so that the workforce can keep pace with competitive and technological changes and spur the organization ahead in innovative, profound ways. Companies have more to gain from a broader, more open program and philosophy in which knowledge, insight, and connections are shared across all levels and departments.

This gets to the heart of modern mentoring. Modern mentoring is a form of open, social, and collaborative learning. Everyone can participate, and people meet in large groups to learn from and share insights with one another. It broadens the scope from one-to-one and top-down connections, and makes them many-to-many and across all levels, functions, and locations. It is typically driven by the needs of the individuals participating, instead of the needs of the organization, meaning that learning is self-directed. It also means that anyone can be an advisor (note that I didn't say mentor), regardless of their job title or tenure, and anyone can be a learner (again, note that I didn't say protégé or mentee). Table 1-1 shows the differences between traditional and modern mentoring.

Table 1-1. Traditional Mentoring vs. Modern Mentoring

Mentoring Program	Traditional	Modern
Purpose	Career advancement	Broad learning
Participants	Mentors are senior leaders and protégés are high-potential employees	Advisors and learners can be anyone in the organization
Connections	One to one	Many to many
Duration	Long term	As long as needed
Method	Face to face	Virtual
Design	Top down and matched by outside administrator	Flat and self-directed

The Building Blocks of Modern Mentoring

The following five core concepts form the foundation of modern mentoring:

- open and egalitarian
- diverse
- broad and flexible
- self-directed and personal
- virtual and asynchronous.

Following these principles will help you get started as you create your own modern mentoring culture.

OPEN AND EGALITARIAN

As younger generations make their way into the workforce, they bring their beliefs and values with them. These can sometimes fly in the face of what organizations consider standard operating procedure, but it does not mean they are wrong. Some of the strongest voices of change come from Millennials who want more openness and equality—both in their personal and professional worlds. This viewpoint plays very well with modern mentoring because for uninhibited and meaningful learning to take place, you must encourage an open environment where people have equal access to one another. Modern mentoring is built on the idea that everyone has something to learn and something to teach. In order to let knowledge flow freely and unimpeded, this type of unrestricted and egalitarian environment is essential.

DIVERSE

Diversity is what will help your modern mentoring program thrive. Here, *diverse* isn't limited to gender, race, and ethnicity it also encompasses learning connections and relationships that cross functional, geographical, hierarchical, and generational lines. Supporting diverse learning connections and participation will help form the foundation of a solid modern mentoring culture. Different perspectives within mentoring communities help novel ideas and approaches arise in answer to problems faced by individuals or the organization as a whole. People in a different functional area or geographical area, or even from a different department or age group, will likely view situations and issues through a distinctive lens and be able to offer a unique perspective and innovative solutions.

BROAD AND FLEXIBLE

Seeking all of your answers and career advice from one person is outdated and inefficient, and I'm not the only one who thinks so. At the 2014 Skillsoft Perspectives Conference, Jack Welch said employees should see everybody as a mentor. He encouraged people to grab the best of what they like in multiple people and run with it, and stressed that we should not get stuck in one person's mold. I agree. No one can possibly know everything, nor are they likely to want to participate in a mentoring program if the expectation loomed that they would have to be an all-knowing sage.

Instead, modern mentoring breaks the cycle of the sage on the stage and pushes the idea of the guides on the side. Learning connections typically occur with multiple people who simultaneously act as advisors and learners, thus forming broad mentoring relationships. People can rotate in and out of these groups depending on who is available and willing to participate. Multiple learning connections and conversations can occur at the same time, allowing someone who is an advisor for one group to be a learner in another group because her level of expertise on the topics at hand will vary. Modern mentoring allows for this type of flexibility so that people can find the right learning connections at the right time, helping them find and apply insights on the job and bring about real results.

SELF-DIRECTED AND PERSONAL

Adults want to drive their own learning. Malcolm Knowles popularized this theory in the 1970s with his idea of andragogy, or adult learning theory. In his book, *The Modern Practice of Adult Education* (1970), Knowles argued that as people mature, they become more motivated to learn based on internal drivers, such as their own personal desire to learn about something, rather than external drivers, such as someone telling them they need to learn about something. He also postulated that as people age, experience becomes an increasing resource for learning, and people seek to apply new insights immediately to solve problems. Jump ahead 40 years and you have the framework for modern mentoring.

People are more likely to be engaged, active learners if they choose what they learn and with whom they collaborate. With modern mentoring, you empower individuals to be in control of their learning and development. Modern mentoring enables employees to address their own personal, real-time learning needs by helping them find, connect with, and gather insights from colleagues from anywhere within an organization. They can gain skills that help them with their own unique work context and make them more productive in a given instance. Moreover, it's not just learners who benefit from this; advisors do as well. They can choose which topics and areas they offer their expertise in, and decide when and if they have the time to participate. This process puts the control back into the hands of the participants and lets them guide their own development.

So how does modern mentoring answer the question, "What's in it for me?" By allowing participants to control the process, they can tailor their learning so that they reap the benefits. See chapter 9 for more about this concept.

VIRTUAL AND ASYNCHRONOUS

Modern mentoring is all about what is right—it pulls together the right people, at the right time, for the right conversations, to find the right solutions for any problems an organization might face. Because of technological advancements, this can be done virtually and asynchronously. The people who would like to connect and learn from one another could be in different parts of the company, different cities, and even different countries. For this reason, modern mentoring often makes use of asynchronous communication and collaboration. Of course, there will be times when synchronous or instantaneous collaboration occurs, but those factors do not have to be present for modern mentoring to work. The growing use of technology for mentoring also means that companies can scale the program and offer it to everyone in the organization at a reasonable price. Viewing mentoring as a practice for the masses will help you harness the collective knowledge, skills, abilities, and passions of your entire workforce.

The Benefits of Modern Mentoring

Modern mentoring can have far-reaching organizational influences, which makes it a great vehicle for engaging and developing all employees in your organization. Some of the benefits you can anticipate a modern mentoring program to have on your organization include increases in retention, engagement, collaboration, innovation, knowledge transfer, and productivity. Keep in mind that modern mentoring is scalable and so are its benefits. The more employees who participate in your program, the wider the positive impact your program will have on your company.

INCREASED RETENTION AND ENGAGEMENT

In *The 7 Hidden Reasons Employees Leave* (2005), author Leigh Branhan states that "mentoring programs have been found to be effective in increasing employee retention in 77 percent of the companies that implemented them." That's an impressive success rate. It's no wonder so many companies clamor to implement mentoring programs. Mentoring can help employees feel more connected to others throughout the organization and allow people to reach out to colleagues for support addressing work-related topics, issues, or situations. Mentoring also makes it easier for employees to navigate career progression options within your organization, be it moving up the career ladder or learning about other functions for a lateral move. Having multiple learning and career options available makes it more compelling for them to stay.

Modern mentoring can also have a large impact on enterprise engagement levels. According to the Corporate Leadership Council's 2011 *The Power of Peers* study, when employees effectively participate in peer mentoring, organizations have seen a 66 percent increase in engagement. High engagement levels are known to increase the number of top performers you have in your organization and the level of loyalty, commitment, and productivity from your employees. Most notably, increased engagement can affect profit. The *Profitable Talent Management* study (2011) conducted by Taleo Research estimated that by increasing employee engagement by 5 percent, an organization of 10,000 employees could boost its bottom line by more than $40 million. Boosting engagement and its associated benefits is one of the many reasons companies are beginning to rapidly adopt modern mentoring practices.

INCREASED COLLABORATION AND INNOVATION

Collaboration between people from different geographies, offices, genders, and generations is essential because it can help spread best practices and critical knowledge across your entire company. Diverse and collaborative learning networks can help employees generate creative solutions, novel ideas, and unique approaches to organizational problems or issues. Broad collaboration can help in several ways:

- People reaching across different generations will gain insights into how people of various age groups tend to think and behave.

- People reaching across cultures can leverage differences to better understand colleagues and clients, and increase creativity and effectiveness when working with people from other cultures.

- People reaching across functions can harness the power of best practices from colleagues in other business units and locations so that they can repeat what works well, rather than trying to invent a new process.

In an era marked by increased competition and rapid change, the need to spur innovation and enable collaboration has never been greater. Modern mentoring can become a key competitive advantage for your organization because it enables this collaborative and innovative behavior.

INCREASED KNOWLEDGE TRANSFER AND PRODUCTIVITY

Transferring organizational knowledge has become increasingly important as more inexperienced Millennials enter a workforce that

Boomers and traditionalists will soon depart. Corporations must seek ways to help older generations spread their knowledge and experience to younger workers who have limited corporate experience and who could learn much from veterans who have years of know-how, best practices, and overall experience in their field. Modern mentoring is a perfect mechanism for connecting the knowledge assets of your organization to help facilitate the development of others. In this way, modern mentoring helps build the capabilities of an entire workforce by increasing knowledge transfer.

Modern mentoring also provides a great way to help create a more productive and effective workforce. In a 2012 study by McKinsey Global Institute, companies saw a 20 to 25 percent increase in productivity in the average knowledge worker as a result of their participation in technology-enabled social collaborations, such as modern mentoring programs. The study also noted that employees spend 47 percent of their work week writing and responding to emails and searching for information internally so that they can complete tasks. Using modern mentoring to effectively source and locate internal information will help free up employees' time for more productive activities. When the impact of increased employee productivity is amplified, it can have a positive effect on your company's bottom line.

CREATING A CULTURE OF LEARNING AND AGILITY

Creating and fostering a culture of learning is important today because it encourages the practice of self-directed learning and development.

In a culture of learning, employees want to proactively share ideas, knowledge, and experience with one another for the sake of mutual benefit and advancement. As businesses become increasingly global and complex, it will be important for employees to collaborate and share best practices so that companies can plug into the collective intelligence of their enterprise. Additionally, it is important that employees look to one another as a resource for learning emerging skills or understanding developing trends. A culture of learning can help employees become more effective at facilitating ongoing learning that is both informal and self-directed. Having an employee base that can quickly respond to changing requirements, skills, and trends will help your organization become more agile. This is paramount, because corporate agility will be a characteristic that defines organizational success as the world continues to change at an extremely rapid pace.

Putting It Into Practice

Modern mentoring can be summed up as mentoring without constraint. It removes barriers, eases administrative burdens, and it broadens the impact mentoring can have by opening up participation to everyone within an organization.

To put modern mentoring into practice and start down the path of building a modern mentoring culture, follow these four guidelines.

Focus on Competencies and Interests

To make mentoring a more practical productivity tool that helps people find the knowledge they need when they need it, the focus should be on competencies and interests. Modern mentoring is about more than just learning from a mentor who can guide your career. It is about learning from everyone around you and applying those insights immediately. Focusing collaborative learning relationships on competencies and interests helps give structure to the group. Employees who want to improve their skills in certain areas should be able to do a quick search for people already using those skills to learn about that competency or capability. Or, if they have an interest in a particular issue or topic, they should be able to affiliate themselves with that competency and show over time that they are contributing to the company as an avid learner or trusted advisor. Either way, the demonstration of a particular expertise forms the backbone of modern mentoring connections and helps give them direction and meaning.

Be Inclusive, Not Exclusive

Modern mentoring should be available to everyone—it is mentoring for the masses. We have to stop selecting a few people for special programs and at least provide a company-wide program that is open to all employees. Special programs too often raise social justice issues and feelings of being left out—no one likes to feel excluded. By creating a broad, inclusive modern mentoring program for your employees,

I suspect you will discover that wisdom, insight, curiosity, and talent have been hiding right under your nose.

Keep Your Purpose Simple

Don't overcomplicate your program by having it address too many things. People will throw around all kinds of phrases to describe mentoring connections—peer mentoring, traditional mentoring, reverse mentoring, group mentoring, on-the-job training, and so on. People may hear reverse mentoring and picture a formal program in which people are hand-selected to participate. The mentor may be younger and the protégé may be older, but not much else changes in that limited view. Can you have group mentoring that is reverse? Do you have to set up programs to support each type of mentoring? Do you have to monitor and lead mentoring groups? Instead of adding to the confusion, I urge you to simplify your message and your purpose. Modern mentoring is about helping people come together so they can learn from one another. It uses technology to do so and removes barriers and limitations found in more traditional programs, but ultimately it is still about learning from those around you.

Advocate for Andragogy

This may be the hardest piece of advice for people to take, but it is one of the most critical. For modern mentoring to work, you have to let people decide for themselves what they want to teach and learn, and make it easy for them to find others who want to do the same. The desire to learn positively influences the commitment and accountability people will have to the group, creating connections that thrive. Taking the power out of the hands of administrators and putting it into the hands of the participants can be a scary thing, but trust that your employees are adults and will know for themselves what they want to learn and if they have time to participate. Your program will hold more appeal because it will honestly represent those who have the passion, desire, drive, and time to participate at that given moment.

Now that I've (hopefully) changed the way you view mentoring, let me help you build your program in a way that embraces the modern mentoring philosophy so you are better positioned to succeed in this rapidly changing world. The rest of the book will provide practical advice and instructions on how to develop a modern mentoring culture—and all the aspects that go along with it.

2

Creating a Modern Mentoring Culture

A few years ago, I was asked to address about 250 organizational leaders at a global pharmaceutical company about the topic of modern mentoring. A senior leader introduced me to the audience: "Joining us today is Randy Emelo, an expert on mentoring and social learning, who will help us modernize our own mentoring efforts. He will show us how to take the practice to the next level at our organization. Mentoring has played and continues to play a huge role in my career and has impacted me at a really fundamental level. I am a true believer in the value and effectiveness of this type of learning. Please listen to Randy carefully. Implementing and broadening the reach of this practice will become critical to our success as an organization."

As I walked on stage, I thought to myself: *Well, that was one heck of an introduction. With support at the top of the house for modern mentoring like that, this company's initiative is sure to succeed.*

And with that I launched into my presentation by asking the leaders to participate in what I like to call the "Ask the Expert" exercise. It is a participatory exercise I use when presenting to an audience on social learning or modern mentoring. Each person gets to play the role of a learner and solicit advice from two other people in the room regarding a work-related problem they are facing. They also get to play the role of advisor and advise two other people in the room based on their particular work-related issues. By having the audience actually participate in this practice, the concept of modern mentoring or learning from others becomes more tangible. It also helps to energize the crowd by igniting the possibilities for the practice's application in their workplace.

And the exercise did just that; the room of leaders was engaged and excited as I began to get into the meat of my presentation—describing what modern mentoring is and how to use modern mentoring or learning networks to support learning and development. As most speakers know, you can typically tell if the audience grasped the message you were trying to get across by the questions they ask and the comments they offer after you finish a presentation. In this particular instance, I took questions from leaders whom I felt really comprehended the larger implications of modern mentoring and how it could be used to support their teams. As I wrapped up my presentation and exited the stage, I was delighted to think that this group of leaders would go out with a solid understanding of the material and use it to really enrich their organization's learning and development efforts.

Unfortunately, my feelings of delight were short-lived. The senior leader who had introduced me came back on stage to thank me for my presentation and to discuss its relevance to the conversation at hand, or so I thought.

Instead, the senior leader dismissed my presentation with this short statement: "What Randy just described to you all is not mentoring." I quickly realized that this leader did not understand or support the practice of modern mentoring and was still enmeshed in the traditional mentoring mindset. My initial delight turned to sobering disappointment. All I could think was: *This is going to be a problem.*

After the session ended, many of the leaders in the audience came and apologized for their fellow leader's comments, legitimately embarrassed by the turn of events. They said that everyone else in the room understood the larger message and believed that modern mentoring would flourish in their organization. They seemed committed to the possibilities available to them through the practice, regardless of the debacle that had just occurred. I am happy to say that they were right; modern mentoring has become the norm for the company and it has been practicing this type of social learning for years now.

Fortunately, this company had leaders who understood and embraced a modern mentoring mindset, but the fact remains that people with antiquated opinions about mentoring can undermine attempts to modernize the practice. You may come across similar hurdles in your efforts to implement the practice. But the good news is that I have some advice to share with you to help you overcome the obstacles you may face. Ultimately, like the organization from my example, you can create a culture where modern mentoring is woven into the very fabric of your organization and social learning is an innate behavior for all employees.

Personal Learning Networks

When people get involved in modern mentoring and social learning, they ultimately build their own personal learning networks made up of the advisors and learners they connect and collaborate with. To help these networks thrive, they must be the right size, shape, and quality.

- **Size:** The core of a person's development network should be between eight and 15 key influencers, with additional people forming outer rings and weaker ties in a broad network.
- **Shape:** A network should consist of learners and advisors from across functions, locations, and generations.
- **Quality:** A network should be diverse, fluid, and dynamic. Participants should be able to move in and out of the network and shift from learner to advisor roles as their learning needs and knowledge strengths evolve.

Just imagine what your organization could look like with personal learning networks like these in action. You could create a thriving learning culture where people take responsibility for their own development and where the buzz of active learning is a constant hum. Now let's get you there. Here are actions you can take to build your new mentoring culture.

Expose Stakeholders

Managers and organizational leaders will likely need to learn what modern mentoring means and why it should be embraced as a valuable development practice. You need to help organizational stakeholders understand the expanded and broad vision of modern mentoring and its associated benefits. This re-education effort will help you eliminate barriers to success for your mentoring program, such as:

- limited and exclusive participant populations
- career advancement and sponsorship as the sole purpose for mentoring
- co-location as a requirement and face-to-face meetings as a primary mode of communication
- assessments and qualifications necessary to be considered a mentor
- mentoring that is only in support of formal programs, such as high-potential development or succession planning.

Lingering perceptions and influencing elements commonly found in traditional mentoring programs need to be minimized in order for modern mentoring to flourish in your organization. To avoid having to combat traditional mentoring mindsets, such as the one the senior leader possessed in my story, start the process by getting managerial and executive buy-in so that you can expand mentoring's impact and push its benefits out to the masses of your organization. Provide them with data that show the benefits of a modern approach to mentoring, and lay out the case to show what is in it for them as organizational leaders. (See chapter 9 for more information.)

Avoid Traditional Mentoring Jargon

To lessen the impact of the multigenerational workforces' perceptions around what mentoring can do or, more importantly, what it cannot do, it's important to use terms that all employees can uniformly understand—despite their generational perspectives. Be mindful that terminology and branding play a crucial role here. I often wonder had I used different terminology to describe the modern mentoring process during my presentation to the leaders I mentioned earlier, if perhaps the senior leader who contradicted me would have been supportive of my ideas rather than opposed to them. To him, the social approach to learning that I described wasn't mentoring. In fact, I've found that mentoring can be a loaded word to use to describe your effort. You might be better served using terminology like *social, collaborative,* or *networked learning* to describe your modern mentoring program. This provides a broader scope to the practice simply by changing what it is called. To further help you, you should aim to position the program as a tool where employees can engage in learning relationships of varying types, from more private and intimate ones focused on career development to large groups discussing best practices for a specific topic. Be sure to provide a solid example of the scope and nature of the learning you aim to support.

Along the same lines, I urge you to stop using the terms *mentor* and *mentee* or *protégé*, and start using *advisor* and *learner* instead. Through their very definitions, *mentor* and *mentee* or *protégé* only offer a limited view as to who the participants can be because mentees and protégés are often associated with people who are being groomed for a specific role by a mentor. To broaden this idea, we need to start referring to people as advisors and learners—and make clear that people can function in both roles depending on what they know and what they want to learn. This distinction is important because it helps lay the proper foundation for understanding the various types of social, open, and collaborative learning people can engage in when taking part in modern mentoring.

By moving to *advisor* to describe anyone who shares their knowledge, we broaden the scope of who can be a mentor. We remove the barriers that surround the traditional ideas of mentoring by introducing the concept that everyone has something they can teach. We all have talents, skills, and knowledge that someone else could benefit from learning. The broader term *advisor* allows participants to easily slip into the role of expert. It also helps set expectations around what role they will play in mentoring groups. They are not there to advance someone's career or become their sole source of advice for years to come; they are simply there for this moment in time to offer advice and knowledge on a specific topic about which they are well versed.

Conversely, by simply using the term *learner* to describe anyone who is seeking knowledge, we can help participants set appropriate expectations as to what they will gain from mentoring. The use of *learner* helps open up people's views on who can benefit from an advisor's knowledge. In traditional mentoring programs, people often see a seasoned employee and assume that person is the mentor in the relationship; yet, that person could be the mentee. In fact, reverse mentoring is gaining ground in organizations as more senior employees seek knowledge and skills from newer and younger employees. Using the terms *learner* and *advisor* helps remove stigma from the idea of being a mentee when an employee has had a longer tenure with the company.

Wrap Modern Mentoring Around Formal Programs

If your organization currently has traditional mentoring programs attached to formal training programs, such as onboarding, high-potential development, or succession planning, these programs can be a great starting place to expand into modern mentoring. Adding the modern approach will mean that the people participating in paired or traditional mentoring can also have the freedom and access to connect with other participants independently as dictated by their own personal learning needs. If your organization's formal programs don't have an accompanying mentoring program, you can simply use the formal program as a launching point for modern mentoring by creating a technology-enabled environment where participants can connect and learn from one another around topics and skills based on formal program curricula or objectives. I recommend a land and expand model: Socialize the practice of modern mentoring with employees who participate in formal programs first (land), and then expand to include other employees at a later date. (See chapter 3 for more on the land and expand model.) You can use the momentum gained in these programs to create a single social learning environment where the whole employee enterprise, from those entering the organization to those poised to exit, can participate in modern mentoring.

With that in mind, consider these suggestions on how to leverage some of the most common types of technologies found in today's companies.

INTRANET

Most companies will have an intranet site that employees can use as a central portal for accessing documents, directories, and important information. If you have an intranet site at your disposal, consider using it to help with your mentoring program.

- Set up user profiles or share employee directories so that employees can use it to look for mentoring and learning connections.

- Create a section for employees to use as an internal wanted section for potential mentoring connections.

- Create a section where employees can post mentoring relationships or engagements that are available for others to join.

- Set up collaboration spaces or communities for group mentoring.

- Allow participants to post information and resources to help drive learning conversations.

SOCIAL BUSINESS NETWORKS

I refer to these social sites as a company's internal version of Facebook, and this is exactly how many employees use them. If you have one of these in place in your organization, consider using it to help with your modern mentoring program.

- Fully utilize user profile features. Ask employees to share their contact information, background, skills, experience, and what they are interested in learning or teaching others on their user profile page.

- Create groups (private and public) that people can use for mentoring collaboration. Allow them to post information and resources as needed to drive the learning conversation.

- Use broadcasting capabilities as a means for people to seek out mentoring partners and publicize popular mentoring engagements to encourage further participation.

MENTORING OR SOCIAL LEARNING SOFTWARE

This emerging technology is a specialized offering that focuses on truly creating a robust modern mentoring and social learning environment.

If you have software like this in your company, you have a huge advantage in creating a vibrant mentoring culture. You can use this software to:

- Leverage user profile information. Encourage employees to include their complete background and learning or advising interests, so mentoring isn't limited to their current job title or role.

- Make it easy to start mentoring. Facilitate mentoring connections based on profile information.

- Foster participation through system notifications, individualized RSS feeds, and so forth.

- Support learning conversations and collaborations through the creation of groups and engagements in which participants can post information, ask questions, schedule events, create polls, and upload resources.

- Gain insight into program participation through reports and metrics provided by the software. Use information about popular mentoring topics and skills to promote further participation.

EMAIL

While some of the previously mentioned forms of technology may not be available in your organization, I cannot think of any company today that does not have email. At the very least, you should have this ubiquitous form of technology available to you to help you build a mentoring culture. You can use email to:

- Help employees communicate across geographies, functions, time zones, and offices.

- Allow employees to reach out to potential advisors and learners.

- Send company-wide updates and promote participation in modern mentoring programs.

Seed the Learning Environment

Conversations that go stale kill engagement when it comes to a modern mentoring learning environment. To combat this, you can take on the role of learning facilitator and help enrich or seed the learning environment by creating groups focused on popular organizational topics and skills, for example "Best Practices for New Managers" or "Microsoft Excel Tips and Tricks." By creating groups on popular topics, you can help drive participation. You do not direct the learning conversation; rather, you enable it. You should recruit advisors to help set learning goals, devise an agenda, and drive the group's discussion accordingly. These advisors can help encourage the conversation by prompting participants to answer a thoughtful question or finding an appropriate resource to spur further dialogue. When new participants arrive to the environment, they will already have a number of pre-formed learning activities to take part in.

Health care company Humana does a wonderful job of recruiting and training their Community Moderators within their Learn @ Clinical Collaborative community. They created a simple document that lays out what is expected of moderators who advise the learning groups (which take place within their Knowledge Exchange social learning software). From listing responsibilities to discussing time commitments, the learning leaders at Humana support their advisors and make joining an easy process. See Appendix II for an example of Humana's moderator support document.

Allow People to Join at Any Time

The point of modern mentoring is to form an ongoing, flexible learning environment. While some may believe that learning should occur within the confines of an arbitrarily defined nine-month formal program, learning does not occur at a preset time. Instead, learning happens constantly, and your mentoring program needs to be set up in such a way that it supports continuous learning.

People will have their own motivations for joining, such as being newly promoted and needing support in their new role, or having a big project to complete and needing to learn about an aspect they are not familiar with. Having a program that allows people to join at any time means that your program will support people at *all* times.

Don't forget that a key pillar of modern mentoring is allowing it to be open and egalitarian. Having an open program means you will need to be able to scale it. To do so, you will need technology in place that makes this cost-effective and manageable, in addition to giving participants a place to go for structured learning.

Engage Your Passive Learners

Regardless of developmental situation or learning topic, an estimated 60 percent of people are passive learners, according to a 2009 presentation from leadership development firm Lominger, part of recruiting firm Korn Ferry. Passive learners quietly take in new information and knowledge, but do little to actively incorporate it into the way they do their jobs. Only about 10 percent of people are active learners, while the remaining 30 percent are blocked, meaning they are completely closed off from learning something new (see Figure 2-1).

Figure 2-1. The Reality of Learning

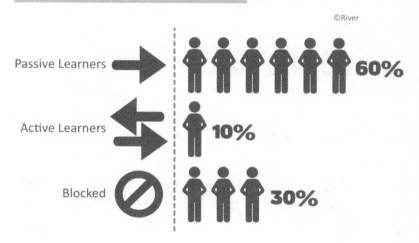

Engaging these passive and blocked learners is critical because when people actively learn, they focus on changing behaviors. Passive learners may learn the right words to say, but they do nothing to actually alter how they work or behave. Even worse, perhaps, are blocked learners who won't even listen, often because they think they already know everything there is to know about the topic and therefore don't have to listen, or because they simply are not interested in the topic. Passive and blocked learners typically don't engage with the information they get through a learning group, interact with people who are sharing their insights, or contribute to the conversation in any meaningful way.

To combat this, tie motivation to learning. Universally, people are driven by individual imagination, passion, and personal experience. Factoring these drivers into learning can help people move from passivity to activity because their motivation to learn is personal. Give employees the ability to choose what topics they pursue for learning, and give them a central place where they can engage with colleagues in modern mentoring and knowledge sharing that is meaningful to each person involved.

Engage Learners Throughout the Employee Lifecycle

Organizations can leverage modern mentoring to support employee development at all stages of the employee lifecycle.

ENTERING

Onboarding is a natural starting place for modern mentoring, especially since many Millennials will continue to enter the workforce in large numbers during the next 10 years. Upon entering the organization, employees of all ages need multiple learning opportunities to help them gain the necessary knowledge to perform their new role. By engaging in modern mentoring and social learning relationships, employees can connect with advisors and other peers who can help them assimilate culturally as well as gain the right insights and skills to help accelerate their speed-to-performance.

EMERGING

As employees mature, some will begin to emerge as natural leaders. Modern mentoring is a great way to support high-potential employees, leadership development programs, and managerial programs. However, instead of limiting who the best and brightest can learn from, organizations can allow these individuals to engage in all types of learning relationships, including those in which emerging leaders can practice leadership skills by advising others or learn from others who have already mastered those skills. Organizations can use learning cohorts or mentoring groups to help make leadership, managerial, or similar training stick by allowing participants to connect with their fellow trainees before, during, and after training. This allows people to learn through each other's applications, successes, and failures with the material or subject at hand.

EXPERT

Once employees have developed to the point of being an expert in their area of focus, they can help facilitate the development of others. Experts can take on the role of advisor and engage in modern mentoring groups to help other employees increase their level of skill in the expert employees' specific areas of mastery. It is, of course, important to keep in mind that experts will span generational, hierarchical, and functional lines, because being an expert in an area doesn't necessarily mean having years of experience. Experts on social media or other emerging trends, for example, are more likely to be found at the bottom of the organization rather than at the top.

EXITING

Modern mentoring becomes a key practice organizations can utilize to capture employees' knowledge before they leave the organization due to retirement or attrition. It can be used in support of succession planning or other programs aimed at sharing the tacit understandings and insights of members poised to exit. Organizations should use modern mentoring as a way to codify and reprocess knowledge held by employees who will be exiting in 24 to 36 months, a timeframe wherein organizations that I've worked with over the years have become concerned about those poised to retire, so that these individuals don't walk out the door with knowledge that may be business critical. Mentoring or social learning groups in support of functional areas of the business, such as understanding a particular product's sales cycle or how research is best gathered for a specific industry, can help not only recycle knowledge, but can also help employees across the lifecycle to learn and develop.

Publicize and Market Your Program

It is important to create great internal marketing that speaks to your organizational culture. It should communicate not only the value of participating, but also how and where to participate. Consider leveraging the following activities to help educate your workforce on modern mentoring, as well as increase visibility of your mentoring program:

- Conduct webinars or e-briefings on mentoring that not only promote current programs, but also educate people on getting the most of their modern mentoring relationships. Help people understand that most of us are involved in informal learning every day, and encourage them to formalize their learning so others can benefit from shared knowledge resources.

- Use various media (podcasts, webinars, and newsletters) to show target audiences how the vision for mentoring can extend beyond a traditional view. By using different messaging with different audiences, you can address their unique concerns and use terminology that will resonate with them.

- Present brief commercials at training events to highlight the benefits of having colleagues with whom participants can discuss what they are learning. This can be as involved as a video showing people talking about how mentoring affected them, or as simple as a single presenter discussing a few stories that helped bring the practice of modern mentoring to life.

- Sponsor roadshows or lunch 'n' learns during which mentoring participants share their experiences. Offering a venue for people to meet and mingle can help energize your program and provides another opportunity for people to network and make learning connections.

- Leverage employee resource groups to help spread the word about your mentoring program. Let already existing networks within your organization help drive and promote mentoring behaviors. These groups can help make learning connections and introductions between employees, as well as help come up with mentoring topics to address.

- Organize town hall meetings during which a brief presentation could be followed by a question and answer session on how modern mentoring has affected people. Use this time to educate the audience on what modern mentoring is, how it can be accessed, and how it can impact participants. Sharing testimonials from participants can be a powerful way to show the process in action.

- Leverage your program's evangelists. If you know certain people have found particular value in the program, unleash the power of a positive review. Urge them to share their experience at an all-company meeting, or use a form of corporate social media to promote their good experience. Even just encouraging your evangelists to share their success story with others around them will help your program gain traction and help encourage further participation.

CASE STUDY: MENTORING VIDEOS AT AT&T

Everything is mobile and personalized these days, and telecommunications powerhouse AT&T takes full advantage of this with two innovative video series: *Morning Cup of Mentoring* and *Mentoring Moments*. AT&T cleverly markets their mentoring program by using technology and media to showcase mentoring in micro-learning snippets.

Morning Cup of Mentoring has fast become a Tuesday tradition at AT&T. Each Tuesday, mentoring administrators post a two- to three-minute mentoring video to their internal networking site. These videos feature midlevel managers from across the business who provide short, practical mentoring tips on subjects that are relevant to the organization's culture, such as knowing the business, AT&T's values, and personal leadership tips. The videos are high energy and engaging, and they provide a hook to AT&T's modern mentoring platform.

Mentoring Moments are five- to 10-minute videos featuring company officers from AT&T discussing broader leadership and cultural topics, such as being your best self at work and building your personal brand. These videos are very popular and provide an inventive way for AT&T executives to spread their insights and share their knowledge with the entire company. This is certainly not something that could be done through traditional one-to-one mentoring relationships. AT&T has found a way to tap into the talents of their leaders to address the evolving needs of their employees.

Reward and Recognize

Employees who participate and contribute to learning conversations and collaborations are a critical asset. These are the people who help build the learning culture at your organization and who provide a positive example of how to engage in learning. Publicly acknowledging their efforts showcases what good learning behavior looks like and encourages others to emulate this behavior.

Putting It Into Practice

Modern mentoring thrives when the entire employee base participates in self-directed learning activities that are motivated by personal drivers. This open and broad approach creates a rich cross-functional, cross-geographical, and cross-generational approach to learning and development that will appeal to a wide range of employees.

Begin to build your culture of learning by answering these questions:

1. Who are my stakeholders?

2. Who are my evangelists?

3. How can I drive participation and interest in modern mentoring?

4. What language should I use that will appeal to my organization?

5. How can I acknowledge the work of those involved?

Use this as a starting point to grow from. Your program can evolve and change over time as more people participate and as new stakeholders get involved.

3

Land and Expand

Mentoring in one form or another likely exists in your organization already. It might be a small-scale formal program used for your high-potential employees. Maybe it's a program supported by your diversity and inclusion team to develop the pipeline to help minorities and women enter leadership roles. Perhaps it's a more informal process that occurs naturally among your employees. Any of these examples can be used as a starting point for a more modern approach to mentoring, or what I like to call the land and expand approach.

The goal of land and expand is to find a natural place to seed modern mentoring within one of your pre-existing programs, and then the concept of mentoring can grow from there. The existing program is where mentoring *lands* as a starting point. From there, mentoring can *expand* as you move the practice forward and push the concepts of modern mentoring to a broader audience.

If you currently have targeted mentoring programs that support formal training programs, such as employee development or succession planning, these programs can be a natural starting place to begin developing a modern mentoring mindset within your organization. Agricultural and biotech company Monsanto used this approach with great effectiveness. "Career development is not defined the same way it was 10 years ago. Employees want access to those who have the skills and knowledge they need now," said Betsy Brennan (2013), learning and development lead at Monsanto.

With this understanding in mind, Monsanto created a modern mentoring approach to address the emerging needs of its workforce. "Mentoring has been an important part of our culture for many years," explained Brennan. "We have a number of traditional mentoring programs going on at any given time of the year within specific leadership, diversity, and career programs. However, as we have expanded globally and grown as a company, we learned that traditional mentoring alone cannot keep up with our need to accelerate development and keep people better connected to one another."

Like many other companies, Monsanto turned to social media as a way to bring people together, but was concerned about the lack of connection back to learning and development. And as I have stressed already, social media can be used as a tool for social learning, but should not be confused with social learning itself. The company chose modern mentoring software as their collaboration platform because it focuses on competency and skill development. "Through specific engagements the learner creates or chooses to join, they get connected to one person or many people who match to their skills needs or career interests," Brennan said. "We, in turn, are able to see where we have competency skills gaps and strengths, as well as how much learning is being transferred across functions and regions."

Hewlett-Packard (HP) also applied the concept of land and expand in two notable ways. First, HP's use of modern mentoring software started out in one function of HP when a visionary leader wanted to offer employees mentoring opportunities to improve their own careers and increase retention. Results were strong, as reported by both mentees and mentors, regarding satisfaction with the program, and more importantly increased effectiveness on the job as a result of program participation. Other HP leaders began to take notice of the data, and the voluntary program and modern mentoring software were expanded to HP's global population of more than 270,000 employees. HP's second application of land and expand was positioning its global expansion of the program and software as part of its existing 70-20-10 development model, initially landing the program as part of its "developing through relationships" offerings. HP continues to identify ways to expand the program and the modern mentoring software to maximize benefits to both employees and to HP.

Program Connections and Ideas

There's no shortage of ideas on how you can connect modern mentoring to existing programs and initiatives. If you already have a mentoring program active in your company, you can simply expand how people view the program, their perceptions on what the program is supposed to achieve, and their mindset on who can take part in the program. The goal here is to help people understand that they can still participate in traditional or paired mentoring relationships if they were already doing so in your pre-existing program, but now they can also have the freedom to connect with other participants independently as dictated by their own unique learning needs or desire to share what they know. A broader mentoring program will give participants the support they need to form their own personal learning network, as previously discussed, and the opportunity to expand their reach. To spur this, start inviting people outside of your program's initial target audience to participate in your new modern mentoring environment.

If you don't have a formal mentoring program in place, there are still many ways you can use land and expand tactics to start facilitating modern mentoring. In fact, this is where we see some of the greatest success when it comes to expanding the scope of mentoring. Many companies launch modern mentoring around an organizational initiative, such as onboarding or diversity and inclusion, and use the emphasis on learning and development natural to these programs to bring mentoring into the fold. Here are some ideas on how you can do the same.

Communities of Interest

With the growing need for collaboration within companies, it's easy to understand why communities of interest are flourishing. Some people may prefer to call these communities of practice, but I believe the word *interest* provides a more inclusive description.

These communities are simply groups of people who share a common interest. They may want to learn more about social media marketing, or maybe their interest lies in the latest coding language. The interest area is what ties members together, rather than their titles or functional roles—as would happen in a community of practice. Communities of interest are more diverse because members come from various backgrounds and with different professional biases and norms.

Communities of interest should be self-forming and topically driven, which will further separate them from communities of practice. Modern mentoring advocates these same factors, helping to form a common bond between the two practices. When you use a modern mentoring approach to support communities of interest, you help build effective learning communities in which practitioners come together to support one another, share insights, test theories, and broaden their knowledge and skills.

In fact, the Corporate Executive Board reports that employees' work today is more interconnected than ever before and this greater interdependence has led to changes in how knowledge is gained and how work gets done (2014). Organizations have a greater need for employees who are effective at improving others' performance and using others' contributions to improve their own performance. Communities of interest are an ideal way to accelerate this critical knowledge exchange.

HP is capitalizing on this important organic knowledge exchange through the communities of interest that have voluntarily formed within the River modern mentoring software tool. HP's top 20 communities of interest include a variety of topics from ubiquitous computing solutions to lean Six Sigma. Even mentoring is one of HP's top-five attended communities of interest.

Diversity and Inclusion

Research has shown that a diverse network can help support deeper learning, spark more innovation, and generate better collaboration. The richness of diverse views and understandings often grows more abundant when people reach outside of their typical like-minded networks. In fact, the more diverse a person's network is in terms of values and viewpoints, the more researchers found that people will increase their performance (Lechner, Frankenberger, and Floyd 2010). Additionally, a 2011 *Forbes* study found that 85 percent of employees agree that a diverse and inclusive workforce is crucial to encourage different perspectives and ideas that drive innovation.

Modern mentoring can fit seamlessly into a diversity and inclusion program for this very reason. Different perspectives within these learning communities help novel ideas and approaches arise to solve work-related and organizational problems. Individuals in a different functional area or geographical area, or even from a different department or age group, will likely view situations and issues through a distinctive lens. Their experiences and focus areas give them a unique perspective, and this fresh take on the situation can produce innovative solutions. Sodexo, a global food services and facilities management company known for its award-winning diversity initiatives, is one of several innovative companies that have decided to embrace the broader view of modern mentoring.

With the support of modern mentoring, you can bring the positive impacts of diversity and inclusion to your entire organization instead of only reaching a small subset of people. Encourage people to use modern mentoring as a way to connect with diverse colleagues and learn from their unique perspectives and attitudes. Embracing diversity can lead to innovative collaboration throughout your organization.

CASE STUDY: SPIRIT OF MENTORING AT SODEXO

Organizations looking to foster and encourage creative thinking among workers, as well as innovative improvements in current processes, would do well to encourage more diversity in individual learning networks. This type of inclusive knowledge sharing thrives at Sodexo, where they actively support learning connections across generational, geographical, and organizational boundaries. They are committed to fostering a culture of inclusion, and their Spirit of Mentoring program embraces a broad approach to collaboration, learning, and development that offers both formal and informal mentoring options.

Using River software, employees throughout the company engage with one another as learners and advisors; transfer knowledge related to their experience, competencies, and needs; and collaborate with colleagues on training, career development, on-the-job productivity, and learning groups. Sodexo makes great use of modern mentoring networks. The following are just a few examples of their internal mentoring groups and programs.

IMPACT: This acclaimed formal mentoring program connects select individuals across cultures and business lines in paired relationships that last 12 months. Administrators match the participants, who take part in a face-to-face program launch and meet virtually with their paired mentor or mentee on a regular basis. In addition to the one-to-one experience, participants engage in a virtual community with the entire group to share resources that hone their leadership competencies. Program metrics based on a longitudinal study show that 42 percent of women involved in IMPACT received a promotion (Davidson 2014).

Peer2Peer Mentoring: This informal mentoring program is made available through nine Sodexo Employee Business Resource Groups (EBRG), such as iGen, an intergenerational group, and WiNG, a women's network group. These EBRGs bring together employees from all areas of the company to connect with colleagues for peer collaboration, networking, and group mentoring.

Expertise in Action: These collaborative learning groups are forming in response to the development needs of the learners within the Spirit of Mentoring system. People can join groups at will and direct their own learning and development. Topics of mutual interest include communication, strategic leadership, and networking, to name a few.

The richness of diverse views and understandings often grows more abundant when people reach outside of their typical like-minded networks. People reaching across different generations, cultures, and functions will gain insights into how people think, better understand their colleagues and clients, and learn best practices from colleagues in other business units that can help them improve their own processes. Diverse perspectives often yield the best business solutions.

Employee Resource Groups

Employees involved in employee resource groups (ERGs) typically have a high interest in networking and collaborative learning. As a result, these groups are a great fit for spearheading modern mentoring and pushing the practice out to their colleagues and connections.

Sodexo is again a great example of a company leveraging an existing initiative as a connection point for modern mentoring. Their employee business resource groups (EBRGs) use Sodexo's Spirit of Mentoring program to reach out to colleagues across locations, generations, and functions. Some of the groups using the program include:

- **iGen:** An intergenerational roundtable group that brings together peers from various generations to share with and learn from one another.

- **HONOR:** A military network group that uses a buddy-system approach through mentoring to help transition former military personnel into civilian and corporate life.

- **PRIDE:** An LGBT and allies group that connects partners for professional development and reverse mentoring.

- **WiNG:** A women's network group that uses topical mentoring in mentoring circles to share, learn, collaborate, and grow with colleagues.

"As our Spirit of Mentoring initiative grows, we continue to see innovative ways to connect people and help broaden learning opportunities for all of our employees," said Jodi Davidson (2014), director of diversity and inclusion initiatives at Sodexo. The company also measures the business-based impacts associated with Spirit of Mentoring.

"Beyond outcomes associated with retention and productivity, perhaps most important is the anecdotal evidence that demonstrates how mentoring has served to raise the confidence and engagement level of its participants," Davidson continued. "There is a natural tie between this and the work associated with Sodexo's employee business resource groups because we know that employees who are members of one or more EBRGs are 61 percent more engaged in the workplace than their peers who are not members of an EBRG. When you add to that the level of engagement when a member is also a partner in a mentoring program, engagement clearly increases."

High-Potential Development

Companies sink a lot of money into developing their high-potential employees. One activity they often spearhead is a traditional one-to-one mentoring program that is hand-matched by administrators. My question to you is: Why limit who your brightest talent can learn from?

Instead of using a prescriptive method that connects a high-potential employee to one mentor, let your brightest talent pull from an array of mentors, advisors, and knowledge resources. This doesn't mean that you have to give up your formal mentoring program if it is working for you, but you should provide these future leaders with a more expansive way to connect with diverse colleagues throughout your organization so that they can build a well-rounded and deep understanding of the business overall.

You should also consider leveraging your high-potential employees as advisors in modern mentoring groups. As your high-potentials gain knowledge and skills, they can share those new insights with their peers and subordinates and gain visibility and experience as a leader. This also helps them build a positive reputations as employees who understand the business and drive for success and openness in their work.

Mergers and Acquisitions

Bringing together companies, workers, and corporate cultures after a merger or acquisition can be daunting. Many workers may quit during this transition because of fear and uncertainty regarding their future. Yet this is the exact time when companies need to retain their employees so that they don't lose critical knowledge or key client relationships.

Using modern mentoring to get through this transition can help organizations successfully manage a merger or acquisition. Employees from newly merged organizations can use modern mentoring technology to meet one another, learn from one another, begin to understand how their combined companies will support one another, and start sharing best practices so that unity and cohesion can form.

Onboarding

What does your onboarding process look like? Is it a series of introductions, a review of policies, a welcome lunch, and a slew of paperwork for your new hire to complete? Does it last a day, a week, or a month? Is it done in isolation through human resources?

The onboarding processes you're familiar with are likely a combination of several of these factors, and not likely to win any awards anytime soon. It typically takes up to 18 months for someone to integrate into an organization's culture. This is much too long. Onboarding is exactly the time when you should be setting the example for the type of culture you have (or strive to have) at your organization, and provide your new employees the means with which to share what they know and learn from their new colleagues.

During their first week of work, you should invite your new hires to participate in your modern mentoring program. Give them the ways and means to get active. This can help them tap into the knowledge resources of your company on day one, which in turn will help to bring them into the cultural fold more quickly and allow them to share their own insights immediately upon hire.

In a 2011 Society for Human Resource Management survey, 65 percent of companies said it is difficult for new hires to learn the necessary information about other people to establish effective working relationships on their own. So, help new hires by implementing modern mentoring and giving them the tools and support they need to establish working relationships. It's within your power to help.

Performance Management

Dare I even tread here, in the land of the dreaded performance review? I don't know of many people who like them or who find the annual version of these meetings helpful. Only 24 percent of managers at U.S. companies (39 percent globally) were found effective at giving employees regular coaching and feedback on their performance, according to the *2012-2013 Global Talent Management and Rewards Study* (Towers Watson 2012). Further, whereas 91 percent of companies sought to use learning technologies to improve talent or performance management, only 20 percent achieved that goal (see Figure 3-1).

Figure 3-1. Percent of Companies Able to Improve Talent or Performance Management With Learning Technologies

91 percent of companies seek to improve talent or performance management with learning technologies.

Only 20 percent achieve this.

Source: Towards Maturity 2012 Benchmark Study

We have to stop making these performance conversations a once-a-year event, and start making them an ongoing, natural part of the workplace conversation. Performance reviews are too often feedback from managers with no tangible means given to employees for improving.

But what if your managers could tell their employees to join a mentoring group? Or what if they could assign them a learning activity within your modern mentoring environment so that the employee could improve while the manager coached from the sideline?

Tying performance management to modern mentoring provides a tangible way for people to work on skill and performance issues as they arise. This allows employees to start improving immediately. People can also capture data on their improvement over time and present it at their next dreaded annual review—I mean, at their next productive meeting.

Retention

People want to work at jobs where they feel valued, appreciated, challenged, and supported. Modern mentoring can play a critical role in creating this type of culture, and can, in fact, have tangible and lasting impacts on retention. I have seen evidence of this at many of our client organizations, through both anecdotal and statistical review. For example, modern mentoring can have a direct correlation on retention factors such as job satisfaction, believing career goals can be met, and feeling that learning experiences and training that can help people be successful are available. In fact, in the early days of web-based mentoring in the mid-2000s, my company conducted research with our clients and found that 83 percent of employee respondents said their mentoring experience had positively influenced their desire to stay at their organization (Triple Creek 2008).

It should come as no surprise that mentoring, even in its modern form, has a positive impact on retention. This type of personalized learning opportunity is what people want, and they will stay in organizations where they get support for their learning efforts and acknowledgment for their achievements.

Sales Enablement

Your sales team is your lifeblood. Without them, business does not close, revenue is not generated, and the company does not stay in business. Yet high turnover, intense stress, and periodic isolation can make the life of a salesperson daunting.

These factors make your sales staff an ideal fit for modern mentoring and social learning. They are hungry for a way to collaborate around pressing problems and to share what they know with their colleagues. In fact, a 2014 Towards Maturity study showed that sales teams are the most likely group (75 percent) to put what they've learned online into practice. The study also showed that 54 percent of salespeople said they find online performance support very useful, and 45 percent said they find external networks and communities very useful.

Give your sales staff what they need. Tie modern mentoring with sales enablement to help sales people share insights, spread best practices, discuss techniques, examine failures, celebrate wins, encourage innovation, and build community.

Succession Planning

Traditional mentoring has always been a key part of succession planning, so connecting a modern approach to this initiative should not be too big of a leap. The key difference is that you will be able to affect thousands of people through the updated approach, rather than just a handful through the more traditional and outdated method.

Think of it like this: You can expand the reach of your top-tier leaders by having them act as advisors to a group of learners. This allows your trusted leaders to share critical knowledge with more than just a future replacement for their role.

Sodexo has seen success with this approach with their Expertise in Action collaborative learning groups, established in response to the development needs of learners within the company's Spirit of Mentoring system. Participants from across the company use modern mentoring software to meet around topics of mutual interest and need for development, such as communication, strategic leadership, and influencing. Survey results show that 85 percent of participants said they can use the learning they gained through the experience back on the job (Davidson 2014). Sodexo is effectively multiplying their functional bench strength exponentially while simultaneously serving the needs of their employees.

Talent Development

Along the same lines of succession planning and high-potential development, a broad talent development approach can be easily supported with a more modern, flexible approach to mentoring. The more people you include, the more talent you expose.

Monsanto provides their employees with access to modern mentoring software that bridges generations, departments, functions, locations, and hierarchy. With more than 22,000 employees located in 70 countries, keeping everyone connected, developed, and engaged is a major factor in their success. "We wanted to reach and develop our talent quickly, so we needed additional ways to connect our people and advance their job proficiencies," explained Brennan (2013). She and her team used River modern mentoring software, which they rebranded internally as Synapse to facilitate talent development by increasing employees access to one another for learning. Modern mentoring software, "fits nicely into how we talk about how development best occurs on the job, and how critical coaching and mentoring are as part of that process," Brennan continued. "With this technology, we can now provide instant access to anyone across the company who has knowledge to share or a desire to learn more," said Brennan.

Monsanto first launched Synapse in the United States and has been rolling it out globally by regions. Monsanto has nearly 20 percent of its employees involved, and the numbers continue to grow (Brennan 2013). "We are now targeting groups that have a higher need for this tool," explains Brennan. "And we will lead facilitated engagements in order to generate higher interest, such as with our new hires, the young professionals' network, and new managers."

Training, Corporate Universities, and MOOCs

Modern mentoring is a great way to extend the value of your training events. You can pull together cohorts for collaboration before, during, and after the event so that they can connect with people as they put theories into practice. This allows you to augment your formal training initiatives (certification-based programs, new manager programs, or e-learning) by giving employees a more meaningful way to connect with one another for learning.

Few people remember all the things they learned during a training session. A 2008 Corporate Executive Board study showed that within a week, people forgot 70 percent of what they learned, and within a month that number jumped to 87 percent. That is a horrible retention rate. But you can help your employees put what they learned into practice right away so that their learning sticks. Peers going through the same training can use modern mentoring to connect and share stories around how they applied the concepts they had learned in class, which will help them retain their newly acquired knowledge. As your learners become more proficient, they can eventually advise future learning groups that form on the topic.

The technology firm EMC did this with their Support New Hire Training course, blending online instructor-led training with a social learning style modern mentoring component. They used River mentoring software before, during, and after their two-week training event to build a learning environment in which newly hired technical support engineers could learn from one another, reference materials from the training course while of the job, and solve customer problems quickly and efficiently.

Modern mentoring allowed EMC's training and learning to be perpetual, and it provided structure for asynchronous online collaboration and conversations. Instructors had a new way to assign work, provide resources, monitor progress, check understanding, and solicit interaction and feedback. Conversely, students could ask questions, contribute to discussions, and document assignment progress. They also saved roughly $270,000 by not having to pay for travel for people to attend a training course in person (see Table 3-1).

Table 3-1. New Hire Training Results From EMC

	With River Social Learning	ILT Only
Final Exam Scores (first attempt)	91.73%	80.75%
Final Exam Scores (second attempt)	95.73%	85.90%
I would recommend this course to others. (five-point scale)	4.84	4.56

	With River Social Learning	ILT Only
This course will help me be more efficient, effective, or productive in my work. (five-point scale)	4.84	4.51
Time saved	Four hours per participant due to pre-work	———————
Money saved	$270,000 due to reduced travel costs	———————

Putting It Into Practice

Now is the time for you to start thinking about how you can bring modern mentoring to your organization. What initiatives would make a good fit for the practice at your company? Where can you land and expand? Where does mentoring already exist? Can you help those participants and stakeholders embrace a broader view of mentoring?

Adding modern mentoring to formal programs is a good way to help it gain traction and continue to expand throughout your organization. Remember that modern mentoring is inclusive, so anyone who is willing and available should have access to participate, regardless of her involvement in a specific formal program. Keep that idea in mind as you start on your journey to bring this practice to life at your organization.

4

Trust in the Social Era

In 1983, I was a young petty officer in the U.S. Navy stationed off the shores of Scotland. The early 1980s represented the late part of the Cold War between the Soviet Union and its allies, and the West. During this time, the enmity between the United States and the Soviet Union had reached a head. While not highly publicized, both nations lived under the threat of a nuclear attack, which could ultimately lead to total nuclear annihilation for both parties. With weapons drawn, each nation waited painstakingly for the other side to blink, to step across the line, to send us spiraling into a catastrophe like no one had ever known.

Israeli historian Dmitry Adamsky accurately refers to the 1983 war games as "the moment of maximum danger of the late Cold War." As a member of the U.S. Navy, I played an active role in this conflict. I oversaw the maintenance and repair of our nuclear reactor systems within our naval submarines. At the time, these submarines, which my team and I worked on, were our nation's forward deployment, or our first line of defense against a nuclear attack. To say that my team and I were busy would have been an understatement. We had hundreds of work orders to complete at any given time, and it was a workload that demanded our full attention and allowed us little sleep or rest.

The omnipresent fear of an impending nuclear war and what that meant for our country and families, our assignment as our nation's first line of defense against such an attack, and the sheer amount of work with which we were tasked left everyone on my team, myself included, overwhelmed, stressed, and legitimately afraid. Tensions within my command ran high.

As the leader of a work center, every morning I would read the day's workload and would call off who was tasked with each project from a list I had created. Each member of my team would respond to my directives with the customary "yes." One such morning, I read the assignments aloud.

"John, today you will head down to the 27 boat and fix that leaky poppet seat on their steam generator. Tom and Kyle, you head to the 32 boat and get to work on work package number 4617."

I continued to delegate work assignments down the line until I got to Gerry. "Gerry," I said, "today you will head to the 24 boat to ship check their new work requests."

But Gerry didn't respond. He looked at me squarely in the eye, but there was no "yes" on his face or on his lips. Five seconds of this excruciatingly awkward standoff continued; to me, these mere seconds felt like hours. Then Gerry broke rank and stepped forward from the line—a sign of defiance and disrespect, and something very out of the norm. The tension was palpable. No one moved. I broke the suspended silence and responded with anger to Gerry.

"What's your problem?" I demanded.

"You're my problem," said Gerry.

Gerry's words hit me like a sucker punch in the face. His response echoed in my ears and stung me to the core. At that moment, I realized that I had a massive leadership crisis on my hands. Instead of powering up, commanding that everyone get to work immediately, and then punishing the defiant Gerry, I told my team to break from formal rank so we could have an informal discussion—allowing them to talk honestly and openly in a safe environment that's free from punishment.

I had been diligently trying to match the right people with the right jobs, trying to shield them from the stress I was under from the higher ups to get the work done. By them not having to deal with the tedious details, I thought I was doing them a favor, serving them as their leader. At my core, I was motivated to make these important work-related decisions by myself, thinking I was making them to increase the overall well-being of my team.

My team, however, did not appreciate this nor agree with the tactic. They saw the situation from a totally different perspective.

They viewed my lack of transparency and authoritative delegations as dishonest, even untrustworthy. Instead of having an energized team ready to work together to achieve our goals, I had a team that lacked any real cohesion. In this mistrusting environment, members of the team moved into a self-protection mode; as a result, they acted primarily in the interest of themselves and not for the team as a whole. I had created a team with no sense of personal ownership of their work, no sense of team accomplishment, and very little team reliance.

I realize now that to the team's and my own detriment, I fell prey to playing the role of the overprotective parent, attempting to shield those I was tasked with protecting from learning life's lessons on their own. In a way, I had taken away the ability for my team to learn how to make critical decisions, how to respond to the results of those decisions, how to learn from those decisions, and how to someday be leaders themselves.

The bottom line: Because I hadn't provided them with a voice or an ability to collaborate around the really important work they knew they were doing, my team simply didn't trust me. We didn't function effectively until I created trust through increased collaboration and participation in our operations, which took time. It was one of the hardest leadership lessons I have learned, but it taught me the following about teams and groups: When a lack of trust and mutual commitment to one another exists, work and learning suffer proportionately.

I tell this story to illustrate how critically important establishing trust is in order for meaningful mentoring and social learning to take place. Your participants in modern mentoring are likely not working together toward making sure our nation is prepared for nuclear war (or who knows, maybe they are), but they are actively working together to meet learning goals. To do this, they need to feel like they can safely share their hunches, ideas, and mistakes. In short, they need to be open and vulnerable. This can be difficult because most of us have career survival instincts that kick in and tells us to shut up so we don't look foolish. But if trust is in place, we can stop worrying about looking foolish and instead focus on learning and improving ourselves.

In today's virtual world, creating this necessary element of trust can be even more difficult than it was creating trust with my team on the ship. Yet it's the new norm for coworkers to be physically distant from one another. If you have an Internet connection and a computer, smartphone, or tablet, you can log on and link up with the office from just about anywhere. However, this physical distance can also make it difficult for some people to trust their co-workers, whom they may have never met. This, in turn, can hamper efforts to create a robust modern mentoring culture; if people don't trust one another, they won't share with one another, and if people don't share with one another, they can't capitalize on the innate value of a widespread collaborative learning process.

Modern mentoring thrives when people share personal, tacit knowledge that is unique to their experiences. This creates a highly contextualized interaction between people, in which knowledge seekers discover how people (advisors and other learners alike) accomplished their work, what they learned, how they overcame challenges, what mistakes they made, and how to avoid them. But if trust does not exist among the participants, then personal and meaningful learning cannot occur.

Asking people to share their personal insights can cause some unease. I'm sure my team of sailors felt uneasy when I prompted them to tell me how they felt about how the team was functioning. I had to break formal ranks to ensure they would communicate with me authentically so that we could collaborate on how to fix our team's problem. Similarly in an organizational setting, participants aren't being asked to simply share a document that their department uses, to which they do not feel any personal responsibility. They are being asked to share information that they gained through their own authentic experiences, which is something much more personal and much more valuable.

These types of genuine reflections and this degree of openness require a certain level of trust between the parties interacting, along with a bit of vulnerability on the part of the person sharing information. No one wants to share something personal, such as their thoughts on why a project failed, only to have their opinions used against them in a different situation. This is why people will typically share common knowledge, but hold back on revealing personal insights in the absence of trust. Yet, these insights are exactly what people need to share in order to achieve effective growth and development.

Understandably, before considering sharing this type of information, people want to know what the receiver is going to do with it.

- Will they share it with others appropriately?
- Will they hoard it?
- Will they use it and then claim it as their own?
- Will they give me credit for what I shared?
- Will they reciprocate by giving information back to me?

In the end, it comes down to this question: How can I trust them?

Some of the most challenging questions administrators may face regarding modern mentoring center on how to build trust in virtual working relationships. Complex questions can arise, such as:

- How do I learn to trust my colleagues in a short-lived modern mentoring group where we may only work together for a week or two?
- How does trust flourish in a multi-person engagement where there are many different personalities and work styles at play?
- Can I trust people whom I've never met, but who are now giving me advice and asking for my help through a virtual mentoring program?

Trust and Virtual Modern Mentoring

Trust must be established in order for modern mentoring to work. Three main factors go into building trust in virtual modern mentoring relationships (and should be present to build trust in person as well): competence, integrity, and caring.

Figure 4-1. Trust-Based Mentoring Relationships

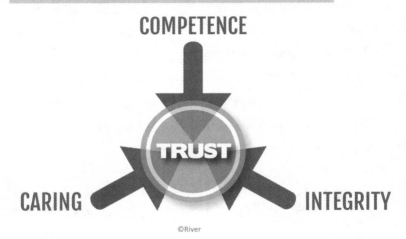

©River

Competence

Trust emanates from those who are good at what they do and who are able to relate that experience to others. While past accomplishments and professional merit contribute to a reputation of competence, in a mentoring relationship competence is demonstrated through the ability to share experiences with others. In the case of my sailors, I was a very competent nuclear welding practitioner, but I needed to show them my competence as a leader in order for them to start trusting me and the orders I gave. I had to illustrate that I could not only understand the work they were performing, but that I could also collaborate with them and share my expertise to help them develop into more advanced practitioners. I learned that for trust to form, I had to show both competence in my area of expertise and competence in the ability to share that expertise with others.

Integrity

Integrity speaks to the wholeness of an individual's character. Those who do what they say they are going to do inspire trust. The same can be said of those who speak truthfully regarding their opinions, thoughts, and experiences. People can show integrity by aligning actions with values and by maintaining confidential boundaries, both of which are vital to mentoring relationships. The first step I took to ensure that my team felt that I had integrity was allowing them to speak freely about what was bothering them. I would not have been able to reestablish trust with my naval team if I had punished those who told me things that were hard to hear. Then, I accepted my error, apologized, and took corresponding actions to remedy it.

Caring

To care means to show concern and interest regarding the needs and desires of others. In mentoring relationships, people exhibit that they care by showing regard for the expressed learning needs and aspirations of others and by actively listening—giving people a safe place to unload burdens and process challenging situations. As I explained to my team of sailors, I really did care about them. My intentions were good; I just had gone about displaying the way I cared for them ineffectively. To earn trust with my team, I learned that I not only had to genuinely care, but that I also had to align the way I showed my care for them with how my team would best receive it. In this case, it was through a much greater degree of participation and collaboration from all of my team members. This is a good lesson for anyone engaging in a learning relationship with others: You must show care in such a way that those you seek to connect with will embrace it.

Competence, integrity, and caring are critical to developing and maintaining trust. No matter how impeccable someone's character is, if they cannot demonstrate competency, trusting them is difficult. Similarly, a competent person who shows no personal interest in your well-being is hard to trust with confidential information. Finally, without integrity, traits of competence and caring would seem inauthentic.

Attention must be given to the actions and conversations that support all three of these dimensions of trust in order to build successful in-person and virtual modern mentoring relationships. (See the practice exercise in Appendix III to help open dialogue between mentoring participants.)

Four Ways to Build Trust

As a mentoring administrator or champion, you can help trust flourish by encouraging people to follow a few guidelines that will build camaraderie and underscore participants' commitment to their mentoring network. All of this lends to building trust and positively affecting engagement in mentoring networks (see Figure 4-2).

Figure 4-2. Improving Trust and Engagement in Mentoring

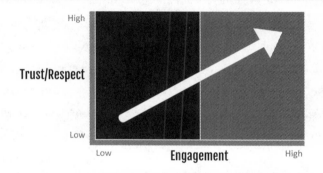

Partially Engaged	Fully Engaged
Limited Sharing	Open/Generous Sharing
Competitive Atmosphere	Collaborative Atmosphere
Guarded/Reserved Attitude	Humble/Authentic Attitude
Focused on Self	Focused on Giving Back to Others

©River

Be Generous

Openly and generously sharing insights and understandings can help establish trust among colleagues and can create a more connected and responsive organization. Motivated by the betterment of others within their modern mentoring communities, generous participants tend to operate out of a deep desire to serve others. They build trust among the group by being highly collaborative, by willingly sharing their know-how, by giving their time and energy, and by referencing the contributions of those they consulted. In order for mentoring communities like this to work, reciprocity must be in place, where people give and take, creating a fluid and graceful dance of sorts with knowledge, insights, and understandings constantly flowing among the group. When one person has a need, others move to fill the gap; when that person has the ability to help someone else in need, they do so eagerly and enthusiastically. A great example of this is when people are onboarded through modern mentoring programs. Employees who have recently completed an onboarding program make great advisors for new hires who are beginning the process because the program is still fresh in their minds. Recently hired employees who have finished onboarding can anticipate the needs of the newest employees, helping them acclimate to the organization's culture.

People who exhibit generosity with their knowledge and time are often seen as approachable, engaging, and thoughtful. They take a personal interest in envisioning and encouraging others to become their best selves, and they seek out opportunities to highlight the positive attributes and unique contributions of people within the context of mentoring. They are genuine, caring members of the modern mentoring community who strive to give back to others around them.

Be Empathetic

Empathy plays a critical role in establishing trust because commitment to one another within the group grows when people consider the perspectives and concerns of those around them. When people show empathy, they project a caring attitude and look at the whole picture to understand how others will be affected. This is important within mentoring networks today because when collaborators can easily empathize with others, it paves the way for open and honest communications—making participants in mentoring programs feel safe when revealing personal information, voicing complaints, or sharing untested ideas. This can help set the tone and work style within a modern mentoring network, providing a positive foundation upon which to grow.

If I had been more self-aware as a young petty officer, I would have realized that my actions were not being seen as empathetic. My team didn't think I had their best interests at heart. To show my empathetic side, I needed to improve my active listening skills and learn how to ask meaningful questions. By engaging them in conversation, I was able to gain a better understanding of the issue at hand, take corrective action, and show my team that I was acting with them in mind.

Be Authentic

People who dare to be authentic in their mentoring interactions take risks, step out of their comfort zone, eliminate excuses, and engage in courageous conversations. These people share successes and failures, and engage in knowledge sharing with a high level of transparency. People need to share what went right and what went wrong so that mistakes are not repeated. It's not easy telling people about my epic fail as a young leader, but I do so with the hope that people can learn from my mistakes.

Authentic collaborators solicit feedback, question their own beliefs based on new information presented to them, and face their failures as learning opportunities. They admit when they don't know something, they ask for assistance, they listen to others in the group, and they show genuine gratitude for the insights they gain from their mentoring cohorts. This helps build a culture in which people willingly share relevant, emerging information that can be applied to real job demands.

A large part of modern mentoring involves revealing personal understandings about what may have gone wrong in the past or what lessons have been learned through previous experiences. Not everyone is willing to communicate these types of insights for fear of being seen as incompetent, unknowledgeable, or foolish. However, when people are courageous enough to let down their guard and expose their vulnerabilities to others, deep and profound learning can occur. As a result, trust is built among participants and commitment grows throughout the group—even if the group is a virtual one.

Be Accountable

To help people feel comfortable enough with their virtual mentoring networks to engage in these types of behaviors, everyone must act with integrity and hold one another accountable. As a mentoring administrator, you need to establish and promote proper standards for these traits so that people know how to act with integrity and accountability when using modern mentoring technology to share knowledge.

Learning administrators at Humana set standards for behavior for participants in their Learn @ Clinical Collaborative group (see Figure 4-3). These speak for themselves, but offer a great example of how leaders can establish a rich modern mentoring and social learning environment that sets the tone for what is expected of participants.

Figure 4-3. Humana's Learn @ Clinical Collaborative Group Behavior Standards

Learn @ CC Commandments

be courteous and respectful of your colleagues

give to the community by posting, not just taking from the posts of others

remember that everyone can see what you post

not post PHI here or on the Knowledge Exchange

not provide any medical advice

not knowingly post inaccurate information

© Humana

In modern mentoring networks, accountability is not just a mental exercise; it involves communicating developmental intents, deadlines, and follow-up among the mentoring collaborators. In a sense, accountability is a learning tool that can be used in every mentoring conversation to ensure that intentions become actions.

To win back trust with my team of sailors, I had to use all four of these trust-building behaviors:

- I had to share my experience and knowledge more readily.
- I had to share with the team that we were all under tremendous pressure to produce, instead of trying to shield them from it.
- I had to become more transparent and collaborative, as well as demonstrate to my team that I truly cared about their development.
- I had to share my mistakes and failures and give honest feedback about my team members' performance.
- I had to hold myself accountable to creating a trusting, cohesive team by committing to create a more collaborative, learning-oriented culture.

The more changes I made to increase trust, collaboration, and learning, the more I saw these behaviors reciprocated by my team. Eventually, the team became comfortable coming to me with real issues or difficult situations they were facing. Not only that, but they began to share amongst themselves more openly and honestly about both their struggles and breakthroughs. As a result, people started discovering and sharing best practices and new techniques that they could apply to their work. Fewer sailors bickered or argued about work assignments, and the competitive nature of our team gave way to a collaborative, energized one. Unlike before when people were afraid of failure, more people were willing to take risks, and an increasing number of my team asked me for tougher assignments to stretch their development. Our productivity started to increase, and we were able to accomplish more with less time and fewer resources than I had initially planned for.

The workplace is not a utopia, but by layering truth and honesty into the foundation of modern mentoring, people can build a community, both in-person and virtually, in which they establish trust among colleagues. Much like I discovered with my team, in a trusting environment, people can create their own little safe haven for learning and personal development and improve the way they work.

Putting It Into Practice

When accountability is high in modern mentoring relationships, you can expect all parties to show up on time, be focused and present (mentally and emotionally), make commitments, and report on results. These attributes do not happen by accident; they are intentional, they take work, and they must be encouraged by everyone—participants and administrators alike.

The following steps can help support accountability within modern mentoring groups. These are written with participants in mind. Administrators can share these steps as a guideline and encourage them to stay accountable to their mentoring networks.

1. **State Your Intended Outcomes.** Describe what you want to accomplish and what actions you are going to take to get the results you want.

2. **Establish a Deadline.** Communicate the date and time when you anticipate completing the action.

3. **Schedule a Progress Report Date.** Hold this deadline as your point of accountability. If the action you are committing to has multiple steps or will take an extended period of time, it is useful to determine milestones that will show progress.

Successful mentoring networks can take concentrated effort and commitment in order to make them thrive. You can help people attain this by encouraging the following behaviors within modern mentoring networks:

- Express mutual appreciation for everyone's knowledge, time, and energy.
- Show willingness to learn from and advise others collaboratively.
- Support the goals, needs, and perspectives of everyone involved.
- Communicate openly and address issues when they arise.
- Encourage feedback to improve competencies and expertise.
- Create a confidential and safe place to learn.

Learning is a dynamic, moving target, with quickly shifting priorities and needs that require a flexible process for gathering insights and applying new understanding. When trust and willingness are in place among modern mentoring participants, unlocking the vault of personal knowledge through mentoring can create a profound transformational experience for all parties involved.

5

Virtual Reputation and Modern Mentoring

In the navy, I had the opportunity to earn the special designation of NEC code 4956, which signifies an advanced specialty in nuclear power plant related welding. But to join and complete the training program required for the designation, I needed to commit an additional six years to my length of service. At certain intervals, the leaders of the program would make cuts based on performance, and those who weren't chosen were sent back to the fleet with a lesser designation. Of the 32 sailors admitted into the program each cycle, only four achieved the coveted 4956 designation. Through a lot of hard work, perseverance, and probably a healthy dose of luck, I managed to survive the cuts and graduate with the 4956 designation. I was proudly sent to a new ship with the immense knowledge this special training represented.

Since the designation was extremely difficult to achieve, there were a limited number of people classified as 4956s in the navy. During my service, there were about 250 of us total. Being a 4956 was like belonging to a fraternity of sorts; we all shared a unique commonality. Due to our ability to perform special duties and functions, there were only a handful of sites around the world that had the complex equipment that required someone of our skill level for service and repair—like the nuclear reactor-powered engines of submarines I ultimately worked on. As a result of our being such a small group, all of the 4956s knew the others' reputations by either working or studying with them directly, or by hearing what others had to say about their character and competence. Reputations became a tangible asset.

Back aboard my ship, I managed a team of practitioners in my area of expertise. At the time, the navy had job rotations of 18 months, so like the tides, there was a constant ebb and flow of people joining and leaving my team. Because this group was all highly competent, most of the prejudgments I made centered on the new person's character, or how they showed up in the past to collaborate and work with their teams at other locations. When I would lose one person, I would use the reputation of the new arrival to plan his work assignments (in a collaborative fashion, of course—I had learned my lesson!) and to determine how to best maintain a positive team dynamic. I'd often ask myself: How productive will this person be? How will he interact with the team? Will he be a leader? I based my decisions for assignments on the person's reputation, from my colleagues' perceptions, and from what I knew about the new team member.

A few times I would be surprised by someone; they would show up and their personality, skill, or work ethic would be different from what their reputation suggested. An example of this was when Garmon joined my team on the ship. Before he arrived, I decided to place him in a key role, because he possessed a reputation for being very innovative, a team player, and a huge asset. We were under immense pressure to produce results, so I waited anxiously for his arrival.

However, when Garmon arrived, I was initially underwhelmed simply because he was quiet and subdued. He was not at all the extroverted, friendly person I had envisioned. Thankfully, despite my initial misgivings, I decided to leave him in the critical role I had planned for him based on his awesome reputation. I'm glad I did! Garmon was nothing short of a superstar. He was able to come up with simple solutions to what had before been considered complex problems. He created what we coined the "gar-bar," a simple contraption that spread pipes. It gave us almost instant access to the hard to reach valves buried among the pipe snakes. We no longer needed to wait for the pipe team to come, disassemble the pipes, and create a working space for us.

The gar-bar is just one example of the innovative work Garmon performed. But it was not just his competence and innovative nature that made him stellar; he was a natural advisor. He helped others around him learn to be more innovative in their thinking and their approach. He taught us to work smarter, which impacted our ability to collectively produce more without using additional resources. While he would have still been a star player on our team if he had kept his knowledge to himself, we achieved huge strides in productivity because Garmon lived up to be the collaborator and team-oriented advisor his reputation presented him to be. I've never met someone whose actions so greatly aligned with their reputation.

Reputation is a powerful thing. It encompasses a person's area of expertise, her character, how she works, and how she shares and learns with others. Within modern mentoring networks, a person's professional reputation can influence whether or not others want to enter into collaborative learning relationships with her. The growing use of modern mentoring and social learning technology necessitates that companies give their employees a way to build and project their own virtual reputations within the web-based learning environment, and to do it in such a way as to ensure it is an authentic representation of a person's capabilities.

The ability to display participants' authentic virtual reputations can take the place of the meet-and-greet phase typical of new in-person relationships, and allows them to jump right into the payoff of sharing knowledge and implementing new skills on the job. The ability to quickly see which employees are engaged in modern mentoring relationships, what strengths they bring with them, and what others have said about their collaboration and work style can help learners and advisors quickly get a feel for their social learning cohorts.

Gaming Principles in Modern Mentoring

The world of online games, such as *World of Warcraft*, can provide many ideas for organizations when it comes to building reputations within a virtual environment. You can discover many innovative techniques from the virtual world of gamers that translate well into the modern workforce. I have found four gaming principles that I support and share with my clients, which can be altered to fit into the corporate world of web-based modern mentoring and social learning.

Principle One: Keep It Positive

While multi-person games such as *World of Warcraft* thrive on competitiveness, running raids, and winning battlegrounds, the virtual world of modern mentoring, social learning, and knowledge sharing flourish best when the focus is on working together, building community, and collaborating with one another. The goal of modern mentoring is that people openly and willing spread knowledge, skills, and know-how among colleagues. This is why it is important for people to have a good reputation within the virtual modern mentoring realm, so that others will come to them for insights and will trust the information and concepts they pass along. A competitive environment can foster distrust and acrimony, making open sharing impossible. People would be more apt to hoard their knowledge in a competitive environment, than generously share their insights with others. Instead, modern mentoring requires a collaborative mindset among participants. This can help build a positive and supportive workplace.

Because colleagues in some organizations never meet face-to-face, using a reputation system built into a web-based mentoring program becomes critical to understanding how people work, share, and collaborate. Three factors should make up a virtual reputation system: a person's expertise, collaboration style, and interests (see Figure 5-1). These should be focused on positive aspects in order to keep the environment collaborative. For example, people could give positive feedback about each other's collaboration style. A common set of positive adjectives such as inquisitive, pragmatic, innovative, or responsive should be included in the modern mentoring environment, and people should be able to tag a colleague to show which aspect they experienced when working with them. Others could see this information when they look at a colleague's profile within the system, providing a leading indicator on what they could expect from that contributor in the future.

Figure 5-1. An Example of a Reputation System

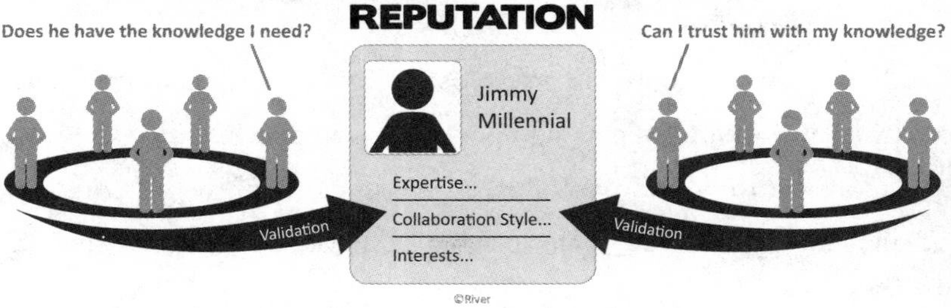

The emphasis on positive aspects helps eliminate negative comments that can create a permanent barrier and hinder knowledge flow, particularly since people may avoid sharing or collaborating with someone who was flagged with a negative remark. Instead, if a colleague does not think someone was very responsive during their previous interactions, they would simply not choose that description. They would focus on what strengths that person did bring to the group and emphasize the positive qualities that person offered to the crowd. Or if more appropriate, they could opt to leave no comments about another's collaborative style whatsoever. Ultimately, a positive-focused reputation system allows contributors' strengths to be highlighted and leveraged.

I was able to put this into action myself during a recent modern mentoring experience in River, the social learning and modern mentoring software that my company both sells and uses internally. In my CEO's Corner learning group, I asked people to give kudos to five other people by selecting from a list of positive collaborative attributes that describe their colleagues and leaving a positive comment for that person. I then asked them to share their reflections on how it felt to do so. What I got back was simply amazing, as the following reflections show:

- "Kind words and genuine praise should not be abnormal to our culture or difficult to give. We create the type of work environment we want to come to every day, and I choose to come to one that is filled with appreciation, gratitude, and genuineness. Thanks to all of my colleagues who help make this company shine!" —Laura F.

- "I love to give others kudos, and I personally feel that the comments section is the key element to this feature. This feature requires the person giving kudos to take time out of their busy day to appreciate and recognize the positive aspects of their co-workers. This also lets the receiver know that their hard work and positive contributions do not go unnoticed on a daily basis. By commenting, rather than just clicking a few buttons, it ensures that the kudos is personal, as well as impactful to the person receiving them." —Chris P.

- "I enjoy giving kudos when it is deserved. I think it is a great way for people to understand how others view them from a professional perspective. That said, kudos may help someone understand more about their strengths than they otherwise would have. In a sense kudos can help us understand how we 'show up' to others." —George B.

I'm really proud of my team and their appreciation for one another. Positivity begets positivity.

Principle Two: Offer Collectible Achievements

Online gamers often collect achievements for performing certain activities within their game. From mining a particular amount of gold to catching a set number of fish, these seemingly small tasks create an impetus that keeps people actively involved in the game.

This same technique can be applied to modern mentoring as a way for learners and advisors to stay active in the program and build their reputation. Personal achievements such as joining a learning group, sharing information, completing a profile, or tagging other users on their collaboration style can be awarded to individuals and shown off to others in a personal virtual trophy case. These award badges help people display their reputations within a virtual mentoring environment, allowing others to evaluate what activities a potential advisor or learner has accomplished and how that might translate into the value that he brings to the learning environment. For instance, people could infer that someone with an achievement for tagging others' collaboration style is an individual who will willingly give personal and meaningful feedback.

Collectible achievements can become a source of personal pride because they acknowledge the endeavors of advisors and learners within the realm of modern mentoring. Giving people a way to positively take part in virtual collaboration and social learning—and recognizing the efforts they make—helps them stay engaged, build their reputation, and become generous members of the learning community. These activities keep momentum going and provide incentive for people to continuously log in, link up, and leverage communal insights.

One important aspect is to let individuals decide what is public and private so that they retain control over their reputation. For example, the following comment from a mentoring collaborator to a participant may be something she wants to keep private: "I am impressed with how well you handled that awkward moment with your boss in today's meeting. I could see you used some of those new techniques we discussed for handling difficult people at work. Nicely done."

While this is a nice and positive comment, it may not be something she wants to broadcast to the world. Letting people choose to keep some comments private is essential for a system like this to work.

Principle Three: Avoid Public Rankings and Numbered Levels

Gamers often talk of leveling up their characters through battles and achievements, meaning that they attain higher levels or rankings based on actions they take in the game. These higher levels come with better equipment, more user features, and improved skill sets. Assigning ranks to players works well in competitive games because it lets people easily see the level of players they are fighting against or teaming up with. However, using this same type of public valuation system in modern mentoring can cause a competitive atmosphere to emerge and can inhibit the very purpose of the group—learning.

Private rankings can be useful because they let people score themselves and track progress when they improve their skills and knowledge. For example, River lets people evaluate their own skill levels around various corporate competencies provided in the program, and then asks people to assign a level for themselves for each competency chosen (beginner, intermediate, or expert) that only they can view. As they improve, they can see their level move upward.

The problem with numbered levels and rankings comes when they are made public, because they accentuate the differences between people and put the focus on labels instead of learning. If competency levels were public, people who are beginners may look for advisors who are experts in a particular competency area instead of considering an intermediate level advisor. Expert level advisors are typically not ideal for a beginner; an intermediate advisor or possibly another beginner who has relatively more experience would be a better match. These people are the ones who can speak the same language as the beginner and can relate to the issues the beginner might face, whereas an expert is typically too far removed from what a beginner is going through to be of much meaningful assistance.

One of the greatest values of modern mentoring is that it removes the barriers people may encounter within the hierarchy of the organization itself. While job title, location, functional area, or business unit may be important distinctions in the physical workplace, none of these matters in a virtual mentoring environment that is open to the entire company. People will simply look for colleagues who have the skills, know-how, and reputation they want in a learning collaborator.

Principle Four: Focus on Expertise

Teamwork is a common element in multiplayer online games. Each player brings a unique skill set that makes her a valuable member of the team. The key is to have a balance of skills among the players so that all areas and needs are covered.

The same holds true within modern mentoring. Learners and advisors who come together through a web-based system need to understand what experience, expertise, and learning needs each person brings. This will allow people to see who needs the knowledge they have, and who has the knowledge they need. When you connect that with the other factors of building a reputation, you provide your participants with a complete picture of who their potential collaborators are, what experiences they bring with them, what expertise they can share, what areas they want to learn about, and so on.

By using a communal set of functional and leadership or management competencies as the basis for expertise profiling, a common foundation forms across functions, departments, regions, and the entire breadth of the organization. This creates a universal framework for learning within the company and helps people connect with the right individuals and groups throughout the organization in order to share critical knowledge. Functional competencies could include aspects related to specific functional domains or disciplines (such as human resources, marketing, or operations), while leadership and management competencies could include skill sets that bleed across functional lines (such as scenario planning, strategic thinking, or time management). Everyone in the system, regardless of their functional role, would see the same list of competencies and use this identical list in order to choose their own areas of aptitude or learning need. This creates a basis for commonality across functions, departments, and regions.

Putting It Into Practice

As I found through engagement within my CEO's Corner mentoring group, giving people positive feedback can be a powerful way to help them build their reputation. You can do the same with your modern mentoring participants by encouraging them to give kudos to others.

I created the following list of positive attributes for you to use and to help you get started. This list represents values that I believe embody the spirit of a good modern mentoring culture and that I urge you to perpetuate within your organization. Use these as a way to help people build their virtual reputations and engender trust.

Ask your modern mentoring participants to choose the top three adjectives they would use to describe one another's collaborative style. For example, "I think of [insert the person's name] as":

- Conceptual
- Decisive
- Supportive
- Knowledgeable
- Pragmatic
- Creative
- Analytical
- Empathetic

- Loyal
- Organized
- Results Driven
- Tactful
- Objective
- Direct
- Friendly
- Innovative

After they have chosen three descriptors, ask people to include personal comments for the individual. The goal is to give people a chance to share genuine feedback and appreciation for one another.

6

Enabling Meaningful Communication and Collaboration

When I was in my 30s, my career idol at the time was a very charismatic and articulate nonprofit leader who influenced the kindness movement and helped shape the notion of pay-it-forward. He was one of the best examples of a servant leader that I had come across at that point in my life. I had always told myself that if I ran into this leader, I would tell him how much I respected and admired his work and how it had always been a dream of mine to work for him. So when I literally ran into him at an industry conference, I told my career idol just what I always promised myself I would. What happened next surprised me.

He said: "Thank you for your kind words, Randy. I can feel how passionate you are about my work. I just created an intern program at my organization whose members I will be working with directly.

If you want to learn my leadership style and come pick my brain, consider yourself invited. So go think on it, and let me know what you decide."

A mere two weeks later, I quit my job and convinced my wife and two elementary school–aged children to move from Connecticut to Ohio so that I could participate in this internship (not the easiest sales pitch I've ever made).

If not already evident by my actions, I was ecstatic. This was a chance to live out one of my professional dreams. I knew that this was the perfect time in my life to develop my own leadership skills, because they would be instrumental to leading the entrepreneurial efforts that already were marinating within me. But I knew I had a lot to learn before I would be developmentally ready to execute my visions successfully.

I arrived and began working as an intern and interacting with my idol on a regular basis. I thought this leader would be teaching me his craft by sharing intimate knowledge with me that would help me emulate his leadership behavior. I thought our relationship would be more personal from a learning perspective. To my disappointment, it wasn't. We interacted often, but I didn't feel that my deep questions were being answered.

That's not to say I didn't learn about being a leader just from having the privilege to work alongside him and observing his decisions and behaviors firsthand. In fact, I learned a lot in the two years that I worked as an intern, and eventually felt like I was ready to go out and start my first entrepreneurial effort. But there was something missing that I could never quite put my finger on.

It was several years later when I learned about the Johari Window, a model for productive communication pioneered by Joesph Luft and Harrington Ingham (1955), that I realized my mistake and why my intern experience felt like a lost opportunity. We all enter the workforce prewired in some ways when it comes to our communication and collaboration styles; nature and nurture enter the equation, and I was not a naturally overt communicator. Turns out, neither was my idol. The reality was that I could have had the intimate and more productive learning relationship I had wanted if only I had communicated differently. Moving forward I realized that if I wanted to make the most out of learning relationships, I would need to be more aware of my own communication and collaboration style and natural inclinations, and then work against them if necessary in order to achieve more productive and meaningful conversations.

Understanding Productive Conversations

Communication and collaboration are the backbone of productive sharing and learning relationships. To make your modern mentoring culture thrive, you will need to encourage productive conversation among your advisors and learners.

In modern mentoring relationships, you want your participants to engage in conversations where they can get to know the people with whom they are collaborating and learn from one another's personal experiences. This will increase the likelihood that learners and advisors generate new awareness and learning through their mentoring activities, and that their efforts will impact their daily work in a meaningful way.

All of us have engaged in collaboration with others and experienced varying results. Some interactions leave us feeling underwhelmed, overwhelmed, anxious, angry, or belittled. Others leave us feeling elated, affirmed, confident, and enlightened. Obviously, most of us would consider the latter to be more productive than the former, and you want to build a modern mentoring culture in which those results become the norm. To help ensure your participants leave their modern mentoring conversations feeling positive and productive, the conversations should contain three characteristics:

- mutual contribution from all parties involved
- constructive banter that allows conversations to flow naturally without a predetermined conclusion
- abundant possibilities that come to light through the conversation.

Productive collaboration and conversations do not end there, however. We have to look within ourselves as well to ensure we are acting as the best communicators that we can. Most people don't realize how much their communication and collaboration styles affect their career outcomes. Had I realized how my passive communication style would affect my time as an intern with my career idol, I would have altered my natural inclination and been more overtly communicative.

Two essential qualities exist in conversations that directly influence how productive communication between people can be: the balance of the dialogue flow and the quality of the connection.

Balance

A balanced dialogue flow occurs when there are equal parts of telling behaviors and asking behaviors. People convey telling behaviors through open and honest expressions of feelings, facts, and guesses in an attempt to share their point of view or understanding. They engage in asking behaviors by actively soliciting information to gain more understanding and insight into their own perceptions and awareness.

In modern mentoring, both the learners and advisors are responsible for ensuring that the dialogue flow is balanced. As an administrator, you may be tempted to monitor dialogue when first building your modern mentoring culture. However, it is best to have a moderator or facilitator take part in each modern mentoring group to help guarantee a productive dialogue flow. Successful conversations within modern mentoring programs often come down to training and laying out expectations for participants at the start.

To help get your participants aligned with good and balanced communication practices, explain to them that everyone has interpersonal communication styles that depend on telling or asking behaviors (see Figure 6-1).

Figure 6-1. How to Conduct Productive Mentoring Conversations

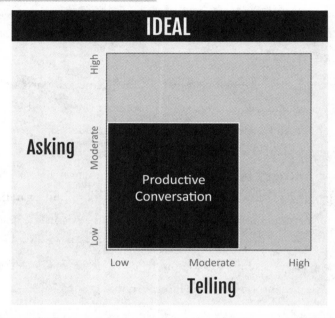

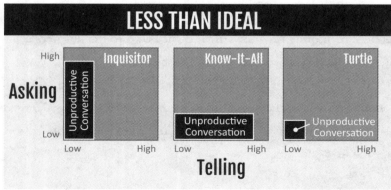

When communications are out of balance, people can ask or tell too much or too little. Unfortunately, unbalanced communications can put forth a skewed view of who they are as a collaborator and make conversations less productive:

- When telling too much, a person can come across as being disinterested in the opinions and thoughts of others, and may appear overly confident in their own opinions. In short, they seem like a know-it-all. This can cause others to have feelings of insecurity or resentment.

- When asking too much, a person can appear to be an inquisitor, hiding behind their questioning and gathering information without the willingness to share their personal insight. This can cause mistrust and suspicion in others.

- When asking and telling too little, a person can seem aloof, disconnected, or disinterested. They may appear reclusive and can cause others to feel depersonalized or devalued.

In my case as an intern, both my leader and I were reclusive when it came to our learning collaborations; neither of us was aware of our natural tendency to under-share. As a result, neither of us pushed the other to ask or tell more, which would have resulted in more personal and productive learning. In order to stretch the edges of productive conversations in modern mentoring relationships, your participants must strive to balance their conversational flow.

Quality

The second factor to consider in modern mentoring conversations is the quality of the connection between the learners and advisors.

Are they personally engaged with one another? Do they feel their collaborators are trustworthy? Are their conversations nondefensive and personally revealing? Or, are they disengaged from one another by a connection that feels impersonal, defensive, and personally incongruent?

It can be challenging for administrators to give up control over who connects with whom, but that is one of the tenets of modern mentoring. The advisors and learners must decide for themselves who they want to connect with, and if the quality of that connection is less than ideal, they must address it themselves. This is a major shift in how most people think about mentoring, especially given the tendency to still hand-match participants in formal programs. But modern mentoring lets people be adults and drive their own learning.

If your participants find that the quality of their connections and conversations need improvement, help them tackle this by suggesting that they try to personally engage in the conversation. To do this, they will need to give voice to their genuine thoughts, ideas, and opinions, which can sometimes be scary. They may need to be vulnerable to their fellow collaborators and let down their defenses, but this openness is critical in forming a quality connection. (See chapter 4 for strategies on achieving trust.) In a productive conversation that has a quality connection, all parties will have revealed a little more of their true essence and gained a deepening awareness of the strengths and abilities of their fellow collaborators.

Developmental Dialogue Model

The best modern mentoring relationships will focus on how to use conversation and collaboration between participants to achieve greater skill or to enhance development. Therefore, it's important that dialogue between participants allows learners to identify opportunities for growth and learning, and gives advisors the freedom to work alongside individuals to help them achieve their goals. To help facilitate more productive conversations, I created the Developmental Dialogue Model (see Figure 6-2). This model uses a cyclical process to move conversations along four milestones:

1. Reflect.
2. Envision.
3. Explore.
4. Act.

Figure 6-2. The Developmental Dialogue Model

©River

This practical approach provides tangible benefits along every step of the way. It enables people to invest an appropriate amount of time in learning the lessons of the past and understanding the current situation (reflect). It ensures that people clearly see and understand the desired outcomes in the future, providing them with a route for both current and ongoing conversations (envision). It offers people an opportunity to discuss options, possible courses of action, and consequences, giving them the time to sort through and narrow down ideas (explore). And finally, it propels people to make a decision, choose a path of action, or take a first step toward a solution (act).

Reflect

Reflective conversations allow people to discuss motivations, search out greater awareness of intentions and future desires, and outline understandings that can help clarify and recap important points as they emerge. This is a critical factor for moving to the next part of the conversation.

Envision

After reflecting on the past and present, it is very important to resist the temptation to jump to an immediate decision. Instead, people should determine what they want the future to look like as a result of their dialogue and collaboration. Shaping an appropriate vision of the future and the desired outcomes creates the trajectory for the dialogue, giving it a sense of direction and movement that creates motivation and engagement.

Explore

People tend to begin their journeys here, without providing adequate time on reflecting and envisioning. It's understandable why people want to immediately explore possible solutions to their problems or challenges, but it needs to be done at the right time and with the right frame of mind. Understanding the past, envisioning the future, and then exploring possibilities and options will help people see the entire picture (including critical elements that could get overlooked otherwise), as well as help them give forethought to actions they may want to take in order to achieve the greatest impact.

Act

The goal of developmental dialogue is change, whether it's a behavior, a circumstance, a goal, or an attitude. Each person's path to change will be unique, and helping people act can be harder than it sounds. Some get stuck trying to find the perfect solution to their problem. Others get sidetracked by minutia and lose sight of the most important aspects of making a decision. During this phase of the Developmental Dialogue Model, advisors can help people determine the appropriate sequence in which actions or tasks should be enacted. They can also provide ideas on how to measure success of these actions.

I encourage you to share this model with your modern mentoring participants. This type of personalized communication has more impact than generic or generalized advice, and it provides a way for participants to engage in productive conversations that align the needs of the individual with the needs of the organization.

People can enter the developmental dialogue cycle at any point along with way. Each step does not need to have equal amounts of time spent on it, but each step should be considered. Once the full process is complete and action is taken, it is natural for people to come back together, reflect on what occurred, make adjustments accordingly, and start the process of iterative learning over again.

The design of this model allows for a deep, developmental approach to unfold with these conversations. Once people complete the act phase, they can circle back, reflect on the outcomes, explore options for midcourse correction, and decide on appropriate actions at that time. People can even condense these steps into one complete conversation so that action is always the result at the end of every dialogue. This kind of communication helps keep modern mentoring conversations open and flowing, moving participants toward collaborative learning that unleashes potential talent.

While participating in modern mentoring, people will move through the four phases of the Developmental Dialogue Model many times and in many ways. The important thing people should gain from this process is being able to look back and see progress in their dialogue, highlighting how they have grown and developed in their understanding of a topic, handling of a situation, or attainment of career skills. To practice using the Developmental Dialogue Model, try the practice exercise in Appendix IV.

Putting It Into Practice

Conversation for the sake of conversation rarely leads to changed behavior. However the reason participants want to engage in modern mentoring is to do just that—change behavior. Engaging in conversations that do not focus on actionable change often gives the illusion of transformation without delivering any actual change in behavior. What ends up happening is that people embrace new concepts and begin calling old behaviors by new names. People feel like they are making progress when in reality they are simply changing their terminology— misapplying new concepts by layering them on old behaviors. This can cause developmental confusion.

Discussing concepts, ideas, and possibilities is an important and valuable aspect of dialogue, but in the realm of modern mentoring, people must also discuss their intentions and end their conversations with planned actions.

Conversations are a means to an end in learning relationships. They help people process concepts and thoughts as they make their way to becoming more effective and productive. It is important to ground our lofty musings (high-concept discussions) with action, thus transforming our thoughts and ideas into new abilities and deeper experiences. I recommend that your modern mentoring participants end every critical conversation with a commitment to undertake some type of specific action. The following conversational strategies will help them as they seek to make their dialogues actionable.

Be Goal-Oriented

Mastery is only achieved through repeated attempts to perfect one's ability or skill in an area of development. Mentoring conversations are greatly enhanced if participants begin and end them with their ultimate objective in mind.

Participant Takeaway: As you consider what action you can take to improve your skill or ability, give high priority to those that will bring you closer to your overall goal.

Be Practical

Personal and professional development is a process that takes repeated effort over time. I've often found that small attempts to take action provide fertile ground for deeper dialogue.

Participant Takeaway: Look to apply your new theory or concept in a common and straightforward way. Take on actions that put the basic principles of your conversation into play and report back to your modern mentoring collaborators regarding your experience and observations in order to stimulate further discussion.

Be a Model

Transformative learning occurs when people apply new concepts and turn them into new behaviors. Had I been more aware of this myself when I was younger, I could have taken action with my idol and gained more from my relationship with him than I did. My passivity held me back.

Participant Takeaway: As you engage in conversations with your mentoring collaborators, consider how the concepts under discussion will affect your current behavior. If you were to adopt a new standard of behavior, what changes would have to take place?

_____

Keeping conversations productive throughout the life of modern mentoring relationships will ensure that advisors and learners gain the most they possibly can from their connections with collaborators. It will also help reduce opportunities lost, like mine as an intern, due to a misunderstanding of communication and collaboration styles.

7

Peer-to-Peer Learning in Mentoring Networks

In 2003, when I took charge of River, I was very passionate and knew a lot about organizational learning. However, I knew almost nothing about the critical aspects of running a business, such as business development, sales, and marketing. I did not know how to manage the finances or how to create a strategic business plan, and I needed to learn about software engineering and coding so that I could manage the people I had hired. I had a vision, but I needed help getting there. It turned out that I needed a mentoring network that I could reach out to for help, information, and guidance.

My network at that time was very different from the one I have today. It has morphed and grown over the years as my needs changed, but I still have a thriving group of peers whom I can call on for advice and share my own expertise with. These are not the same people I started out with all those years ago, but that is to be expected. My needs today are not the same as they were 12 years ago. I am now much more adept at business development, sales, and marketing, which means I can now share with others who are beginners or less experienced than I am in those areas.

I've had to put work and energy into my network throughout the years, and it has not always been easy. Sometimes getting started can be the hardest part. Approaching that first person can seem daunting and fear of rejection can hold you back. I've had people say no to me over the years, but I've found that most people genuinely want to help. If they can't answer your question, or provide you with assistance at that time, they typically try to point you in the direction of someone who can.

Creating a broad mentoring network that can shift with your needs and gives you a place to gain skills and share your own knowledge is critical.

Supporting people as they grow their mentoring networks ties back to one of the most critical questions facing learning and development leaders today: How do we develop workers for jobs in which the knowledge, competencies, and relationships needed change constantly?

Answering this question requires stepping outside the box of traditional mentoring. Senior leaders from numerous organizations have told me they need a more connection-based learning model that allows people to:

- Engage in self-directed learning.

- Increase their speed to competency.
- Create adaptable and flexible development networks.
- Learn in collaborative ways across functions, levels, and geography.
- Share and generate new ideas.

In short, what learning leaders are telling me is that they need their employees to engage in peer-to-peer mentoring networks.

Think about your own organizational environment. Could you find value in a process that gives people the power to direct their own learning, increase their speed to competency, create their own flexible learning networks, collaborate across boundaries, and generate new ideas? Of course you could.

In 2010, one of my clients, a large multinational technology firm, surveyed their River participants to find out how people were using the system and who they were connecting with for mentoring. Of the more than 5,000 people surveyed, they found that 46 percent of self-directed learning relationships occurred between people at the same job level. These mentoring participants chose to learn from their peers almost half the time. For the remaining relationships, 19 percent were reverse mentoring, in which a person in a higher organizational position looks for an advisor who is lower in the organization, and 35 percent of the connections were traditional, meaning someone lower in the organizational hierarchy sought out a more senior advisor.

The shift from a traditional connection to a more peer-driven relationship highlights a growing trend: More people are seeking insight and information from their direct colleagues rather than from a supervisor or senior leader.

Five Reasons for Peer Connections

Why do people seek out their peers when they want to learn new skills or are building critical competencies? What are the benefits of peer-to-peer mentoring networks? How can learning leaders support these networks so that knowledge sharing can flourish?

Several reasons exist for the recent growth in peer-to-peer learning and mentoring. Understanding some of these reasons, such as contextual understanding, similar outlook, diverse perspectives, and social support, can help you position this new learning opportunity in the proper way.

Availability

Subject matter experts (SMEs) are not the only people who can be advisors. In fact, if you only use your SMEs as advisors, you will have difficulty finding enough people to be advisors. I've seen it time and time again. There are just not that many SMEs available.

But, if you look at expertise as a continuum upon which people can have different levels of proficiency, you will have a vast supply of people who can be advisors. This opens the door to having advisors who are peers (or even subordinates), and not always having to go to the extreme expert as your advisor.

An extreme expert typically does not make for the best advisor to someone who is a beginner. Beginners need advisors who are only a step or two ahead of them in terms of proficiency. They need the advisors who can show them the basics, teach them a few tricks, and give them a process to follow as they build their skill area. Your extreme experts should be free to advise those who are more seasoned practitioners on the expertise continuum, but who have not yet achieved expert status (see Figure 7-1).

Figure 7-1. Expertise Continuum

	Beginner	Practitioner	Expert
Learning Focus	Know the rules	Break the rules	Make the rules
Functional Base	Knowledge	Understanding	Wisdom
Application	Unreliable	Selective	Spontaneous
Comprehension	Low	Adaptive	Intuitive
Judgment	Limited	Conscious	Discerning

©River

Concepts adapted from Dreyfus, Hubert L., and Dreyfus, Stuart E., 1986

Contextual Understanding

During the Information Age, the primary focus was on gathering and making content available. Organizations worked to codify their knowledge, push their data out into repositories, and then make that data available to anyone seeking it. To see this in action, simply Google "knowledge management" and watch the millions of results that come up in a fraction of a second.

However, this type of knowledge gathering has outlived its usefulness when looked at in terms of building competency among the workforce. No longer is person-to-content the main focus of people's learning needs. In today's knowledge economy, workers need less generalized content and a more relevant understanding of how to apply knowledge on the job.

Information overload is a common reality in our lives. How can people know which piece of data is best suited for their circumstances? More people are using a micro-learning approach by collaborating with people in their network around a short abstract, video, or skill brief. This lets people shift from drowning in too much content to focusing on quick application of targeted knowledge in the right context. Learners have their skill needs met by being able to apply the right information in the proper context of their jobs.

Similar Outlook

People in a company who share a similar title are organizational peers; for example, managers in various departments can be considered managerial peers. They may work in different functions, but they have similar responsibilities.

These peers understand the pressures, realities, limitations, and expectations associated with a certain level of responsibility in the company. Because of this, they make ideal advisors for people in similar roles.

Peers can bring new insights to learning relationships that someone at a different organizational level may not have. They can also provide the right context when discussing work-related issues with each other because they experience comparable situations. This comes into play particularly when making plans to meet organizational goals.

Everyone needs to plan for the future to some degree in order to do their jobs well. According to Elliott Jaques' time span of discretion theory, the higher up in the organizational hierarchy people rise, the more responsibility they have. Those responsibilities will differ in terms of what type they are and how difficult they are as people rise through the ranks. Consequently, the higher employees rank, the farther ahead they need to exercise foresight and plan for future scenarios, contingencies, and situations, such as the need for new product lines, anticipating workforce growth, preparing for changes in overall market demand, and so on (see Figure 7-2). For example, senior leaders typically plan three to five years ahead because their responsibilities revolve around integrating systems throughout an organization. Middle managers look roughly one to two years ahead because their responsibilities center on creating the systems that people will use. Supervisors have a future vision that sees about nine months ahead because their responsibilities lie in areas associated with managing the work of others and making sure work gets done, and individual contributors look ahead roughly one month out because their responsibilities focus on doing the work.

Figure 7-2. Foresight and Planning Required for Different Employee Ranks

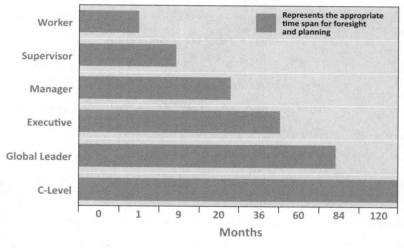

*Model based on the work of Elliott Jaques
©River

Given these realities, a learning relationship with someone at a different level could produce confusion, misunderstandings, and frustration. Peers who hold the same level of organizational responsibility plan into the future to the same degree. As a result, engaging with people at the peer level allows conversations, ideas, and plans to fit appropriately with the learners' needs. These peers can speak in terms and ideas that each other understands. Peer learning connections allow for productive conversations and planning to occur because advisors and learners approach issues from the same position and with a related mindset.

I've encountered this myself with my own network. I am part of a CEO group that meets to share knowledge, address problems, and support one another. My fellow CEOs and I face similar challenges, even though many of us run companies in different fields. This common foundation and perspective can help me talk through issues with people who get it. I've found their support to be invaluable over the years.

Diverse Perspectives

As more organizations strive for innovation in a global market, the focus inevitably turns to diversity. The push today is not just for more diversity based on age, gender, race, or ethnicity. The drive for companies today is to foster more diversity of thought by bringing together people from different functions, locations, and divisions. This diversity of perspectives is what will drive innovation. People will bring with them their various experiences, work styles, and insider knowledge, which they can then share with their colleagues as they work to solve real business problems.

I find that connecting with peers from different backgrounds can provide me with a unique perspective. In my CEO group, we are all organizational leaders, but we operate in different fields. We all face similar issues, but we approach them differently.

For employees you may be supporting with new modern mentoring networks, this distinction means that cross-functional peers can also seek out one another to gain a fresh perspective on an issue. These colleagues may encounter similar problems when trying to execute plans, but given their functional expertise, they may have unique ways of approaching the situation.

If you ask the same question the same way to four different people from four different backgrounds and levels of experience, you will likely get four different answers. I've discovered this myself with my own personal mentoring network. My network includes advisors from the construction, financial securities, environmental engineering, predictive analytics, nonprofit, and human capital software industries. When I consult them, I know that they will give me their best advice based on their knowledge and experience—and this is exactly what I hope to gain.

For example, a supervisor in customer service may be able to share new ideas on client interactions with a supervisor in marketing. These colleagues have the same level of authority in the organization, so they understand similar pressures and expectations due to their roles. However, because their expertise areas differ, cross-functional peers can help one another innovate, brainstorm, generate ideas, and gain fresh or unique perspectives.

The large multinational technology firm I mentioned earlier found that 56 percent of mentoring relationships in their organization were cross-functional. Additionally, 29 percent took place across geographies through their global enterprise mentoring program. Many companies have started using modern mentoring as a way to foster a global program that forges connections across locations. This broader approach increases openness and diversity within organizations.

Social Support

One of the most valuable perks I get from my CEO peers is not advice, but rather an open ear that listens without judgment. I'm sure you can relate to that. I don't always want an answer or a possible solution; I just want to share my frustrations or air my concerns. Knowing that I can do this within the safety of my network makes all the difference.

Peers are often the best sources for social support because they face similar situations and comparable expectations. For example, team leaders from various departments can collaborate with and support one another through company transitions, projects, annual reviews, and giving feedback. They can encourage one another in a way that no one else can because they are living the same reality and with the same daily pressures.

Organizations that provide ways for peers to connect and share with one another in learning relationships can positively influence engagement and can combat feelings of isolation and underappreciation. In fact, the *2014 Recognition Trends Report* by Quantum Workplace showed that access to new learning and training opportunities is the second most desirable form of recognition for engaged employees, coming in only after a pay increase.

A pay increase is not always feasible, but there is a way for companies to show their appreciation and give employees what they want: modern mentoring opportunities. By providing the structure, tools, and software employees need to build modern mentoring networks, you will positively affect their engagement, giving them a way to gain social support and helping them increase their competency and skill.

Putting It Into Practice

Organizations that operate on the assumption that only experts should teach or advise others are missing the power of peer learning to increase their employees' competency. Providing ways for peers to connect in modern mentoring and social learning relationships across the enterprise can help them build support networks and increase the flow of knowledge throughout the organization. Leveraging the power of peer-to-peer learning can help create better contextual understanding for learners, give them access to advice from people who understand their position in the organizational hierarchy, allow them to see another point of view that is relevant to their work, and can help create peer networks for ongoing support as people strive to build similar competencies and skill sets.

As you start putting this into practice, help your employees understand three principles outlined below on forming positive peer relationships within modern mentoring networks. This will help them create a foundation for success.

Look for People Inside and Outside Your Discipline

If I had only looked for advisors within my fields of organization development and learning when I became CEO of River, I would still be clueless on how to actually run a company. Instead, I looked beyond my discipline and found advisors who could help me learn about finance, business strategy, sales, and more. This broad approach was critical to my success.

You have to encourage your employees to branch out and look for connections in all areas of the company. Don't allow barriers—real or imagined—to hamper exploration and innovation. Instead, provide the tools to support employees in their efforts and give them ways to easily build a vibrant network.

Create a culture in which there are no obstacles to collaboration and diverse views are appreciated and celebrated. You could even start by using your own network as an example of how diverse, collaborative relationships work.

Share What You Know

I think of learning as a cycle. As I acquire new skills and knowledge, I also take time to share what I know with others. This becomes an easy and natural occurrence in a thriving mentoring network. I have insights and opinions that I can share with people on various subjects, just as there is plenty I still need to learn from those who are willing to share with me.

People can upset this cycle by only taking from others and not giving back in return. You can address this by setting the right expectations. As you develop a modern mentoring culture in your organization, be sure to set guidelines for behaviors that can be shared with all participants. In chapter 4, I shared how Humana put this into practice by creating commandments to follow within their Learn @ Clinical Collaborative community of practice in their Knowledge Exchange social learning environment. These short, clear, and easy to follow instructions, such as "Give to the community by posting, not just taking from the posts of others," ensure that everyone adheres to the same principles for collaborating. Bottom line: Hoarding is not healthy.

Beware of the Herd Mentality

It's been said that people with power often find themselves in an echo chamber surrounded by yes men. They are told only what they want to hear, and are rarely presented with unique perspectives or contrary opinions. This is a dangerous situation to be in.

While we aren't all power players, this can still happen in our own networks. One of the main values found in modern mentoring networks is that they consist of multiple people who bring with them different outlooks and viewpoints. The moment everyone in your network starts agreeing without any dissension is the moment when you may want to look at bringing in new peers. Don't be afraid to let your network flex and grow. Invite some fresh voices that can give you a new way of looking at issues.

A Generational View

The funny thing about modern mentoring and peer networks is that younger generations view this as the way life works. This isn't a radical concept to them. They've been sharing online and collaborating with peers since they were children.

I've had many conversations with people about generational viewpoints and differences, but the best way to put it is to sum it up with this fictionalized conversation.

A Candid Conversation on Mentoring With a Millennial

Randy Emelo: Jimmy, let's get to know you a bit. Why don't you tell us about your career so far?

Jimmy Millennial: Career? I don't think about my work in those terms exactly. I think of it more as following my interests, passions, and abilities and seeing where it all leads. Maybe that's here, maybe it's somewhere else. But I don't necessarily have a career plan in mind that lays it all out for me for the next 30 years.

RE: So, then, you would not view mentoring as primarily a way to advance your career in a formal sense?

JM: I want to learn from others, and I value the wisdom of older, more experienced people. But I don't see mentoring as a stepping stone or a ladder I use to get ahead. I see it as a way to follow my interests, to learn, and build a network of people I can bounce things off of.

RE: So for example, who exactly would you want to connect with right now if you could?

JM: Well, I'm really interested in using social media in a different way with our clients and have some ideas that I think could make a difference on our reputation out there. But, I've got no idea where to start. I'd like to connect with others working on similar problems to collaborate.

RE: Why don't you just talk to your manager about your ideas and let her work it up the chain?

JM: In the two years it takes for an idea to work its way up the chain, the social media environment will have changed and the tools I'd like to use may be obsolete. We will have missed a great opportunity to communicate and bring value to our customers right now. I need to be able to bypass the organizational hierarchy and connect with people so I can both learn from and share knowledge with them. That's how I view mentoring. It's a two-way street: We should learn from one another and collaborate on issues that make a difference.

The bottom line: Millennials want to learn in this more open, accessible manner, and they will do so with or without our help as organizational leaders. It behooves us to get involved in the process and help make this type of learning and mentoring work so that we can harness the skills and creativity of *all* the generations of our workforce.

8

Modern Mentoring and the 70-20-10 Learning Model

A wise person once issued me a warning when I was young. He told me that you are the smartest you'll ever be when you graduate high school, and the dumbest you'll ever be when you graduate college.

Now, as a young man, I certainly thought this person was way off the mark. How could I not be smarter once I finished college and attained my degree? That would be four more years' worth of learning, education, and information that I'd have acquired. By all accounts, I'd be smarter, right?

In some ways, yes; I would gain knowledge from my education. But in other ways, the person who gave me that advice was right. I'd be book smart, but not necessarily experience smart.

When we exit the educational world and enter the professional one, many of us quickly realize that the material we learned in school provides a solid foundation for our careers, but that we still need experience with the practical, hands-on application of that knowledge. My son, Todd, went through a situation like this when he first applied for jobs after graduating from college. Armed with a computer science degree, he was easily able to secure interviews as a desirable candidate. His first-round interviews were a breeze; he had all the concepts and theories mastered and answered all of the interviewers' questions well. But when he got to the second round of interviews, things did not go so well. The interviewers would ask him to write code on a whiteboard or to show some behavior to demonstrate that he could perform the work at hand. The issue for him at the time was that he had never applied the theories and concepts of computer science in a real business situation before. He lacked the skills to take school-based knowledge and put it into practice in a real-life scenario. Eventually, Todd found a job as a junior developer, and I can proudly say that he is a very talented developer today.

However, many people have faced the difficult transition from learning to doing. The fact remains that some skills and knowledge cannot be gained in a classroom or from a book. Moving from school to work can make this extremely apparent.

Think about how you conduct training and support learning at your organization. Most organizations follow a traditional classroom model that uses an instructor to dole out information to a group of learners, or they may have modernized the practice by using e-learning to shuffle people through training sessions. Often, these training models fall short of helping people put concepts into practice. These programs fail to give participants the tools they need to practically apply their knowledge. Learners need social and experiential learning to augment their formal learning.

70-20-10

Researchers at the Center for Creative Leadership (CCL) popularized a model of learning in the 1980s and 1990s that showed how 70 percent of what people learn is through experience, 20 percent is through exposure (such as learning through other people), and 10 percent is through education (such as through books or formal training). This is now known as the 70-20-10 spectrum of learning (Figure 8-1; Lombardo and Eichinger 1996).

Figure 8-1. The 70-20-10 Model

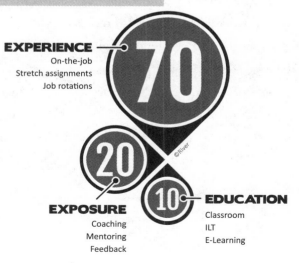

EXPERIENCE
On-the-job
Stretch assignments
Job rotations

EXPOSURE
Coaching
Mentoring
Feedback

EDUCATION
Classroom
ILT
E-Learning

Michael Lombardo and Robert Eichinger, from the CCL, published the model in their book *The Career Architect Development Planner* in 1996, and the concept has spread and grown since.

With this model in mind, where would you think organizations spend the majority of their money and resources? Would you believe that typically 90 percent of a learning organization's effort is focused on education and formal learning—which is just 10 percent of the learning spectrum? Think about it: The majority of the learning in which our employees engage is not being influenced or supported by our organizations.

The educational sector of the model provides a good way to deliver compliance training or very basic skills, but it is not how many of our employees learn or how they want to learn. More than 100 years ago, when workers simply needed step-by-step instructions to complete repetitive tasks, formal training made sense. But in today's rapidly changing work environment, this model is outdated.

To bring learning and development into the modern era and to support the needs of today's knowledge workers, organizations must find ways to support the entire 70-20-10 spectrum of learning, not just education and formal learning. Modern mentoring can be an underlying support system that enhances learning activities throughout all areas of the 70-20-10 continuum. Here's how.

Widen the Impact of Education and Formal Learning

Just 10 percent of learning comes through educational efforts. So savvy companies are maximizing their formal learning efforts by creating modern mentoring or social learning cohorts used in conjunction with training and other types of learning. These organizations tap into the more social and hands-on aspects of the 70-20-10 model and make use of the entire spectrum of learning by having structures in place that allow people to connect with their modern mentoring cohorts before, during, and after a formal training course. This lets people get to know one another before the training or course begins, interact with one another during the course, and continue conversations after the course is finished. Colleagues can then seek one another's support when they are back on the job implementing the new theories or practices they learned in class. By supplementing training or other formal programs with modern mentoring, you can expand learning activities beyond the end of the course or event and help participants apply new skills on the job.

CASE STUDY: EMC—21ST-CENTURY BLENDED LEARNING

At EMC, a major technology company in the data storage industry, they leveraged social and informal learning to support formal technical training classes. They embrace the blended learning best practice of learning cohorts, mentoring groups of classmates who collaborate before, during, and after formal training to help cement new learning.

Participants in their Support New Hire training course were asked to virtually connect and collaborate with a group of their classmates around trainer-led discussions before the actual in-person portion of the training session. This saved EMC four hours of classroom time per participant and allowed them to focus on essential in-person engagement. EMC's learning cohorts helped enhance the overall learning experience for participants and improved retention. Participants were encouraged to continue collaborating and discussing real work-related applications of their learning after classes concluded.

Since participants had built relationships over the duration of the class, their modern mentoring groups became a virtual sounding board in which they could seek feedback from peers, ask questions about experiences and challenges, and discover best practices for applying new learning on the job. By building peer relationships before and after training courses, EMC extended the learning that took place as a result of their more formal initiatives by tapping into social and experiential learning modalities.

Fully Leverage Your Employees for Learning

Twenty percent of what people learn comes from exposure and learning from other people. This section of the model is where mentoring typically appears; however, traditional or paired mentoring is the most common way I've seen organizations apply this. They are missing out on so much by failing to implement modern mentoring.

As I've discussed throughout the book, traditional mentoring is a largely ineffective practice and is just the tip of the iceberg when it comes to organizational social learning. Unlike rigid one-to-one pairings, the flexible and dynamic learning relationships of the modern mentoring practice are designed to help employees with whatever work-related issue they currently face. As such, the more people who take part in modern mentoring, the more knowledge and experience you can make available to employees. As that pool becomes broader and more diverse, you can build a culture that embraces learning networks that adapt to meet people's needs and maximize social learning at your organization. Open, collaborative environments devoid of restrictions or barriers work best for social learning because they allow people to come together to learn from one another's experiences and to share highly personalized information and knowledge. In order to maximize the impact that can occur within the exposure portion of the model, be sure to go well beyond traditional or paired mentoring and enable modern mentoring (see chapter 2).

Tap Into the Experience of Your Workforce

The bulk of learning (70 percent) occurs through hands-on experience and informal learning opportunities. This likely doesn't surprise you, but it might frustrate you as you try to figure out how to harness, measure, and expand upon this fact. Modern mentoring can help in that regard because it provides the structure you need to capture and share what people are doing when they are learning on the job. Modern mentoring also supports learning and acquiring new skills and knowledge in the context of a person's day-to-day work through targeted collaboration with others. Because modern mentoring is focused on helping individuals accomplish learning as their work demands, the sum of individuals learning new skills and building new competencies can positively impact knowledge growth across the enterprise.

Modern mentoring can support experiential learning by giving people a place to reflect on what skills they attempted to apply and connecting them with a group of people who can help them try new options. For example, a sales team that is applying a new technique on the job could use modern mentoring to discuss the technique, examine failures, celebrate wins, and encourage further innovation.

Rarely will one intervention allow someone the opportunity to learn what they need to adopt a desired behavior or achieve a particular result. Learning occurs over time as people discover something new, attempt to put it into practice, and learn lessons from each attempt.

In fact, reflection over time is known to increase learning retention by up to 22 percent (Di Stefano et al. 2014). Modern mentoring takes advantage of these realities and treats learning or a reflective process, rather than an isolated event.

Holistic Learning at Xerox

For more than half a century, Xerox has been a leader in document technology and services. It employs more than 140,000 people worldwide and holds more than 12,000 patents. The company is dedicated to innovation and spends a portion of its revenue each year on research and development.

It is within this environment that Xerox created Xerox Services University (XSU) and began using social learning and modern mentoring technology to support a range of client services in areas as diverse as healthcare, transportation, and IT and HR outsourcing. XSU was designed to provide a way for all employees to develop the competencies, skills, and learning relationships needed for individual and organizational success. The company also built a commons area within XSU that uses social learning technology to support modern mentoring, collaboration, and peer coaching.

XSU is a progressive example of how to maximize learning by exposing participants to formal, social, and experiential learning, regardless of the driving force behind the learning need. Xerox used the principles behind the 70-20-10 model as a guideline for structuring the university and its learning and development offerings. The university is a single learning environment in which formal learning efforts are enhanced by informal, social, and experiential learning opportunities. These three learning modalities work hand in hand to introduce, support, and reinforce each other.

Xerox embraced and championed the main pillar of modern mentoring: All employees, regardless of age, tenure, or role, can be learners in one area, while simultaneously acting as practitioners, teachers, coaches, advisors, and mentors in other areas. Formal learning makes up part of XSU's overall curriculum; however, Xerox recognized that the most valuable organizational knowledge resides in the minds and experiences of its employees, not in course content. It was with this understanding—and the fact that modern mentoring can help enable learning that spans the entire continuum—that modern mentoring was built into the foundation of XSU.

Through the commons area of XSU, Xerox offers its employees a central place to learn, a means to connect with colleagues across the organization, access to online courses and content, and the freedom to take charge of their own learning and development depending on their individual needs and aspirations.

To help participants easily locate and engage in appropriate learning opportunities, Xerox created schools that use pre-formed modern mentoring groups and corresponding curricula. These schools create a path for employees to follow; guide participants through a learning process that incorporates formal, social, and experiential learning; and addresses their overall level of proficiency. Five schools currently exist within the university:

- The School of Creativity and Innovation equips Xerox leaders with methods, processes, tools, and techniques to think and work creatively and drive innovation, ultimately providing valuable products and services to their customers.

- The School of Operational Excellence provides Xerox leaders with the principles, practices, and tools necessary to achieve process excellence and build a culture of continuous improvement.

- The School of Leadership equips Xerox leaders with the tools and resources to engage and develop teams, establish a shared vision, inspire and motivate others, and continuously improve team performance to achieve business goals.

- The School of People Management enables Xerox leaders to develop the interpersonal and organizational management skills necessary to motivate individuals and teams toward accomplishing strategic business goals.

- The School of Business Foundations equips Xerox leaders with the business acumen about financials and sound decision making to drive Xerox's sustained profitability and growth.

Each school centers on a unique focus and provides the structure that employees need to advance their careers and build new skills. The courses and authoritative content contained in each school connect to the focus of that school, but since people can follow multiple paths at once, cross-pollination of ideas, content, best practices, and policies will occur. This further builds and supports XSU's overarching goal of a holistic learning environment that uses all methods and means available.

Putting It Into Practice

Looking back on the past 60 years, it is interesting to note that while technology and the concept of work have rapidly advanced, organizational learning and development has somehow managed to lag behind. While today's work environment looks nothing like that of the 1950s, the way that most organizations support learning and development is tragically outdated, straight out of the Industrial Revolution.

Organizations may fool themselves into thinking that they have advanced their practices because they use 21st-century technology. Yet, despite the emergent technology used to support it, most organizational learning is still based on formal, Industrial Age learning methodologies, resulting in offerings that are based on one-time events and one-way knowledge transfer. To make learning an activity that actually equips today's employees to be successful at their jobs, organizations have to modernize their mindset and approach to learning. Consider these three main movements of the modern workforce to get started.

From Conformity to Creativity

Today's fast-paced, ever-changing business world calls for employees who envision new possibilities and who operate as flexible contributors, rather than as Industrial era workers who simply completed their assigned tasks the same way. Now, learning must become less conformist and classroom-based and more collaborative so that it can inspire creativity and innovation. To do this, organizations should stop focusing on doling out knowledge, and instead create environments that foster inventive and productive learning through targeted dialogue and engagement with others.

From Information to Wisdom

The average worker has instant access to almost unlimited sources of information. Unfortunately, access to information doesn't necessarily help people learn what they need for success on the job. For that, employees need wisdom or the ability to apply knowledge acquired from others. Wisdom is gained from other practitioners who can share their successes, failures, and experiences. Static e-learning courses, traditional in-person classes, and other formal learning activities provide information but struggle to help people attain wisdom. To have a greater impact, learning should be based on the context of the learner's job, not just fixed content or one-time courses.

From Generalized to Personalized

For knowledge workers, one size does not fit all when it comes to learning. Skills are in the process of constant decay, which demands a more personalized and continuous approach to on-the-job learning and development. In fact, a commonly stated statistic claims that the skills and knowledge of the modern employee are often only relevant for 12 to 18 months. Workers have to constantly keep up with new trends and emerging skills to stay relevant. To help learners significantly increase their speed to competence to stay relevant, organizations must build a learning environment that actively recommends personalized and process-oriented learning opportunities spanning the 70-20-10 continuum.

The Xerox Services team embodies the shifts in the modern workforce by encouraging innovation and giving employees the ability to take part in learning activities across the 70-20-10 continuum through XSU. Their employees may not realize how groundbreaking XSU is because all they see is that their knowledge needs are being met when they need them to be. The epitome of good learning is when it doesn't feel like learning. By using the 70-20-10 continuum as part of your modern mentoring program, you can give your learners and advisors a seamless learning experience by continuing to provide learning opportunities beyond traditional classroom-based training, giving them multiple ways to put learning into action to address performance, and by aligning their learning environment with business strategies. The Xerox Services team has differentiated themselves and XSU from standard corporate training and learning initiatives by being willing to embrace an open, collaborative learning style. By integrating modern mentoring into your formal programs, your organization can also adopt a more innovative learning culture.

Figure 8-2. Education-Based Learning vs. Experience- and Exposure-Based Learning

Education-Based Learning

Learners are limited to the information the certified instructor teaches.

Learning is unidirectional.

Experience- and Exposure-Based Learning

Learners are connected to large, global knowledge networks, making learning nearly limitless.

Learning is multidirectional.

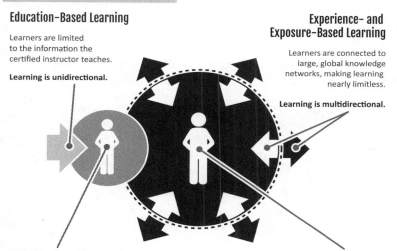

Traditional Worker

Conforms well
Knows the facts
Committed to job
Competitive
Follows directions

Modern Worker

Creative and imaginative
Makes wise judgments
Relationally connected
Generous to others
Questions status quo

Success is:

Concrete
Measured by testing
Shown through basic information and skills learned

Fluid
Measured by creative use of knowledge
Shown through willingness to share knowledge and overall job success

©River

9

What's in It for Me?

After examining the various aspects of modern mentoring, we now come to the quintessential moment when you ask yourself: "What's in it for me?"

I was reminded of a striking what's in it for me (WIIFM) moment in my life during a recent family gathering. Most of the older men on my father's side of the family worked at least a portion of their careers—if not their entire careers—in mining, manufacturing, or a similar industry. As a result, seemingly everyone on this side of the family lives with the unfortunate reality of being hard of hearing.

While my career path was different, I was not immune to a noisy work environment. During my service in the navy, there was no shortage of noise that could damage one's eardrums. Ships and shipyards are not typically quiet places. As a result, the training manuals said to wear protection on your ears, especially when performing activities that can cause hearing loss. But I was in my 20s and thought I was invincible; plus, putting in earplugs was just another step to take to get the job done and I didn't want to be bothered. So I welded, cut metal, and did my work, ignoring safety instructions.

Maybe it was a family trait to ignore the rules, because I seem to have plenty of relatives on my father's side of the family who had similar thoughts in their youth. For whatever reason, I did not follow the safety precautions when it came to protecting my ears. Well, as you can likely guess, I paid for that massive lapse in judgment.

Every year in the navy, sailors go to the doctor for an annual health evaluation, an event I never really gave much thought to since I never had any serious health conditions. During one particular evaluation, that all changed. I went in feeling confident that I was in great physical health and had nothing to worry about. I'd be in and out in no time.

But after my exam, the doctor told me we had to talk and asked me to sit down. Dread settled in my stomach. This was not a good sign. I thought to myself: Doctors only ask you to sit and talk if something is really wrong. The doctor went on to explain that I had already lost 35 percent of my ability to hear. Ironically, I heard him very clearly when he delivered that news. He told me that if I continued to ignore the instructions to wear earplugs during loud work activities, my body would be unable to heal itself and the damage to my hearing would become permanent.

This was a sobering encounter and I took this doctor's advice very seriously. After my evaluation, I always wore my earplugs for fear that

I would lose my hearing if I didn't. I should have just followed the rules that were clearly outlined during my training, but I was a cocky kid who thought he was tough. It was easy for me to ignore the safety standards because I didn't fully understand how I could be affected. I didn't grasp what was in it for me.

This experience taught me—and continues to teach me—that most people must first clearly understand the answer to WIIFM in order to take a desired action or follow specific instructions. This may frustrate us sometimes as learning and development practitioners who are trying to provide opportunities to people for training and learning, but I get it. We've all been guilty of WIIFM moments. Think about a time when you had to be convinced of something, when a colleague or a friend had to practically give you a 20-point synopsis to bring you over to their side.

Now think about the times when you've been on the other side of the situation, trying to convince a boss or a peer to take part in your initiative. Did you help them understand why they should? Did you show them what they would get out of it on a personal level? What if you proposed a modern mentoring program to your organization? Do you feel prepared to show them what's in it for them?

It can be maddening to have to go through the steps and appease people, to have to come up with numerous arguments about why they should do something that you know is truly a great idea and would be good for them. But when you step back and look at it from the participants' perspective or from your executive team's point of view, can you blame them for asking?

We are all strapped for time, energy, money, and resources of all kinds. The thought of trying to squeeze one more thing into our already busy lives can seem insurmountable. But if you frame it correctly you will create a culture where people seek out modern mentoring and social learning opportunities, and where you gain the explicit support of leadership and your executive team. You won't have to explain why people should want to take part or why they should provide funding; they will start coming to you to find out how they can join and how they can make this work.

This happened at Sodexo. The Sodexo team took the time to understand what its associates were looking for when it came to personal development opportunities, and then tailored the messaging to show how the Expertise in Action social learning groups could meet people's needs. From showing a correlation between modern mentoring and on-the-job productivity, to highlighting costs savings, it was able to make the WIIFM connection for individuals, managers, and organizational leaders.

"In the past, we would need to actively pursue people to participate in mentoring," said Jodi Davidson, Sodexo's director of diversity and inclusion initiatives (2014). "Today, business partners within our organization are initiating opportunities to leverage mentoring and our Expertise in Action social learning groups to advance their areas of focus."

Xerox accomplished this as well when promoting the benefits and value propositions for Xerox Services University (XSU) and the affiliated commons area that houses the integrated social learning functionality. By tailoring XSU's WIIFM value points to leaders at various levels within Xerox, administrators gained support and buy-in from these critical partners and participants. The Xerox team was able to show how XSU would positively impact each level of their leadership structure, while also showing that unifying themes exist among the three audiences.

For organizational leaders, administrators pointed out that XSU provides:

- A valuable tool to improve employee engagement.
- A means for organizational leaders to connect with participants and teach them business needs.
- Opportunities to network, collaborate, and build their competencies and skills while on the job.
- A tool to manage and monitor strategic business change.
- A means to expose the unique contributions and talent of employees that might otherwise go unnoticed.

Administrators explained to departmental leaders that, in addition to the above, XSU provides:

- A curriculum of micro-learning courses designed to help develop their skills and competencies as they develop their career as a leader.
- An opportunity to support and learn about strategic business changes.

For first-level leaders, administrators pointed out that XSU provides all of the above, plus a clear demonstration of organizational commitment to their development.

What Are Your WIIFMs?

As you bring the expanded approach of modern mentoring to your organization, you need to identify the various segments of your audience and the value propositions that are going to resonate with each. In chapter 1, I briefly discussed how modern mentoring positively affects areas such as retention, employee engagement, knowledge transfer, and productivity. Now I will arm you with additional information to help you prove what's in it for your participants and stakeholders.

Participants

Participants in modern mentoring can be learners, advisors, or both. They can be from any location, division, function, level, or role within an organization. As such, you may need to segment your audience into several categories and alter your message accordingly. I recommend that you ask for help from your internal marketing or communications team to provide you with assistance and guidance. This type of audience segmentation is typical for marketing, and you would likely be able to tap into their expertise when trying to take on this task for your initiative.

Some of the key benefits of modern mentoring for participants include the ability to:

- Connect and collaborate with any employees in the organization.
- Leverage personalized learning so you can succeed in the workplace.
- Get up to speed on emerging topics and trends.
- Find colleagues and build learning networks that fit your unique needs.
- Be empowered to direct your own learning and development.
- Get help understanding your career path, options, and opportunities.
- Learn new skills or expand existing talents.
- Engage in modern mentoring to solve problems and perform better.
- Select the competencies you want to gain knowledge on.
- Act as a sounding board for colleagues as they test ideas and plans.
- Share insights, spread best practices, and encourage innovation.
- Discuss techniques, examine failures, and celebrate wins with a diverse group of colleagues.
- Get feedback on your professional and personal development.
- Accelerate your development and growth.
- Share your expertise and experience with others.
- Enhance coaching, communication, and interpersonal skills.
- Translate values and strategies into productive actions.

- Assist in the transfer of knowledge among peers at the organization.
- Help in the development of others.
- Learn about the organization and current business issues.
- Discover new truths and pioneer new methodologies.
- Develop and demonstrate leadership skills.

Organizations

A 2013 Towards Maturity study showed that 94 percent of organizations want to speed up the application of learning back in the workplace, but only 19 percent are achieving this. I believe we can do better.

Modern mentoring is the tool we can use to bring personal, practical, and active learning back to the job. People want to learn from one another. In fact, the same Towards Maturity study reported that 86 percent of employees said they are learning what they need to know for work by collaborating with others. Let's use this desire and proclivity to learn from one another to our advantage. (Curious about what Millennials want? See Figure 9-1 to learn what this generation is looking for.)

Figure 9-1. What Millennials Are Looking for From Their Jobs

DID YOU KNOW?

The opportunity for personal development is the top factor that influenced Millennials' decision to accept their current job.

Training and development is the top benefit Millennials most value from an employer.

Source: PwC, "Millennials at Work, Reshaping the Workplace," 2011.

3 out of 4 Millennials would like to have a mentor.
Source: MTV Research, "No Collar Workers," 2012.

8 out of 10 Millennials want regular feedback from their boss.
Source: MTV Research, "No Collar Workers," 2012.

2/3

Two-thirds of Millennials think they should be mentoring older co-workers on technology.

89% of Millennials think it is important to be constantly learning at their job.

Source: MTV Research, "No Collar Workers," 2012.

MOST VALUED

Which training/development opportunities would you most value from an employer?

28%	6%	5%
Working with strong coaches and mentors	Formal classroom training	E-Learning

Source: PwC, "Millennials at Work, Reshaping the Workplace," 2011.
©River

169

With modern mentoring, organizations can:

- Identify and close skill gaps across the entire enterprise.
- Positively influence areas such as employee engagement, retention, and productivity.
- Gather business intelligence.
- Improve workforce effectiveness in a swiftly changing business environment by enhancing skill development linked to business goals.
- Cultivate creative leaders.
- Build effective learning communities where practitioners come together to support one another, share insights, test theories, and broaden their knowledge and skills.
- Enable peer-to-peer collaboration and learning.
- Keep proprietary content and knowledge resources in-house.
- Personalize learning by connecting it to people's daily work.
- Reinforce training through critical modern mentoring and social learning conversations and collaboration.
- Reduce costs of formal training.
- Demonstrate your commitment to developing employees.
- Build diversity in your pipeline.
- Find hidden talent.
- Turn your subject matter experts (SMEs) into learning facilitators.
- Help your SMEs share what they know with vast numbers of learners.
- Gain evolving insight into employees' emerging areas of interest.

Managers and Supervisors

Researchers at the University of British Columbia found that people with greater access to experts accumulated significantly more skill than those with less access, and they retained their skills for much longer. For managers and supervisors, this type of skill attainment and retention is exactly what they are looking for when it comes to developing their direct reports. The difficult part is that formal training takes time and money, both of which can be hard to come by. In addition, 88 percent of learners want to be able to learn at their own pace, which can make it challenging for managers and supervisors who have to compel people to attend a formal training course (Towards Maturity 2013).

Rather than fighting this uphill battle, managers and supervisors should look to modern mentoring as a way to give direct reports the type of learning support and collaborative environment they want, while also being able to use it as a way to manage and measure progress for their direct reports. For example, managers could enroll their direct reports into a modern mentoring program to help them learn about emerging trends so that they can stay on top of the latest ways to effectively do their jobs. Participants can then discuss these trends with their peers in other locations, departments, or functions so that they can hear from people with different perspectives and experiences.

Another way managers can use modern mentoring is to enroll direct reports into mentoring relationships to give them a way to work on development needs specified in a performance review. This lets the managers and supervisors provide input on the performance coaching that their employees need, and lets the employees know that their managers are committed to helping them improve.

The reasons why managers and supervisors might enroll their direct reports into modern mentoring tie directly to the benefits they might see. These benefits include the ability to:

- Gain insight into competitors.
- Discover new methods, processes, and procedures.
- Spread best practices among departments.
- Expose employees to people in the company who can help them.
- Provide a more formal career development relationship for direct reports.
- Supplement training and formal learning efforts.
- Address performance issues.
- Identify future leaders.
- Build a team culture that values support, sharing, and partnership.
- Demonstrate your commitment to developing employees.
- Support cross-functional communication, teamwork, and learning.

The benefits of modern mentoring are plentiful and can be deeply personal. Whether you are a participant, organizational leader, manager, or supervisor, you can use modern mentoring to enable micro-learning opportunities, personalize learning by connecting it to people's daily work, and reinforce training through critical social learning conversations and collaboration. Just think: These benefits and value propositions can multiply as your program grows.

Putting It Into Practice

Now that I've shared some of the benefits that can come from modern mentoring, let me ask you this: What is your vision for modern mentoring at your organization? Whom do you want to involve? How do you want to introduce the practice? Where does it fit naturally? Who are your champions and stakeholders? Whom can you lean on for support?

As you begin thinking through these questions, a picture will begin to form. It will show you the depth and scope of your ambitions when it comes to implementing modern mentoring at your organization. It will also help you clarify who your participants, stakeholders, champions, supporters, and influencers are. Once you have these people identified, you can project your vision and show them what they can gain by being a part of this endeavor. This is the point at which you can begin to express the WIIFMs for each group you've identified.

Having specific audiences in mind will help you craft an individualized message that will speak to each group. However, there are several broad concepts related to modern mentoring that you should keep in mind as you draft the WIIFMs for each group. These are all concepts I've already discussed throughout the book, but I want to reiterate them here.

- Empower employees to direct their own learning so that it aligns with their immediate needs, particularly within a rapidly changing business environment.

- Encourage cross-departmental and cross-organizational learning opportunities, which can help foster creative solutions and leverage different perspectives.

- Allow modern mentoring to occur in an open environment where people have equal access to one another.

- Permit people to shift in and out of the program—and of the learner or advisor roles themselves—as learning needs and knowledge strengths evolve.

- If piloting a program, be sure to use a group of people who have a true need to collaborate to give an accurate picture of what the program can achieve.

So what do you say? Are you ready? I think you are. You can do this! Take that first step and get started.

CONCLUSION

Into Action

I recall, some years ago, sitting in an auditorium after hearing a very inspiring and personally challenging message. As I was basking in the warm glow of inspired thought, the speaker said something that I have never been able to forget. He said, "The deep things in life are the simple things, profoundly experienced." As everyone was furiously scribbling this profound statement in their seminar booklets, I was internalizing the importance of this thought. I was dumbstruck with the realization that I had been listening to this inspirational message with no thought of its implications to my life. Instantly, I went from being comforted by the logic of the speaker's argument to being troubled by the radical changes that would need to take place in my personal life to make the ideals in his message come to fruition. Simply stated, I needed to move out of my head and into action.

If some of the thoughts I have shared cause you to think differently about mentoring and its potential impact on your organization, then there are two important things to consider:

1. your personal learning orientation

2. the readiness of your organization to embrace the practices of modern mentoring.

What Kind of Learner Are You?

As I discussed in chapter 2, learners fall into one of three categories: active, passive, or blocked. Only 10 percent of us are active learners, while sadly 60 percent of us are passive and 30 percent are blocked. Think about all of those people furiously scribbling down that profound statement we heard at the conference. How many of them do you think took that insight and did something with it? Turned it into an action? Made a change based on what they learned? Or how many of them wrote it down, smiled and nodded as they thought about it, then closed their notebook and never gave it another thought? I'm willing to bet most of the attendees did the latter.

What would you have done? Would you be willing to challenge yourself and make a real change based on new insights? Would you be open to doing so when it comes to modern mentoring?

Think of it this way: What kind of learner are you?

Blocked Learners

Blocked learners are not open to learning anything new about a subject. They either disagree with the point of view being presented, or they are not interested. My thoughts and opinions on the modernization of mentoring practices will only serve to reinforce the current views of a blocked learner. There is very little that will sway one who sees no value in exploring a different way of thinking about mentoring.

Active Learners

Active learners take in new information while considering how it will change their behavior. Simply stated, they listen with the intent to do. They are constantly focused on improving their effectiveness. The new concepts and practices I described in this book will serve as a model of behavior for active learners. They will immediately envision radical changes that need to happen in order for modern mentoring to take shape in their organization.

Passive Learners

Passive learners seek to understand new concepts as an end unto itself. They are perpetually taking in new information and relating it to their current behaviors, changing their language but not their actions. Consequently, old behaviors simply get new names. The new concepts I presented will cause the passive learner to consider calling their current mentoring activities by new names.

In summary, you probably had one of three internal responses to my challenge to you to modernize your mentoring practices. You will either want to dismiss it as irrelevant, overhaul your learning systems, or rebrand your current mentoring practices. Where do you land?

Organizational Readiness

People often ask me how they can tell if an organization is ready for modern mentoring. When I created the first known e-mentoring software system 15 years ago, this was a difficult question to answer. The discussion often turned to issues like the technological acuity of the workforce, computer access, lost work time, and security protocols. Thankfully, most of those issues are irrelevant today, given the technological advances and ubiquity of social media and the Internet. Most workers today have access to the Internet through portable devices, social collaboration has been proven essential for workforce performance, and many of the security issues have been addressed by maturing security protocols.

What we are left to contend with is the prevailing attitude of those in charge of the corporate culture. Is your organization willing to support a new way of learning? In my experience, organizations will fall on a continuum of willingness that goes from resistant to receptive (see Figure 10-1).

Figure 10-1. The Continuum of Organizational Readiness

ORGANIZATIONAL
READINESS

Resistant   Receptive

Conforming culture ---------------------------- Creative and imaginative

Abundance of hierarchy ---------------------------- Agile organization

Strongly siloed ---------------------------- Highly collaborative

Technologically rigid ---------------------------- Technically diverse

©River

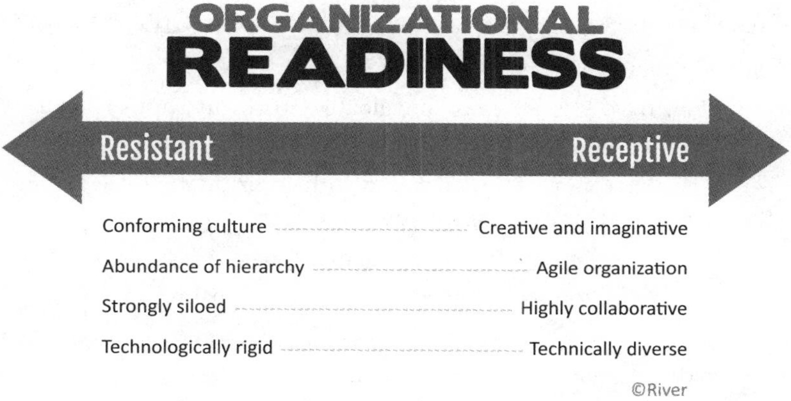

Resistant

Organizations that are resistant to modernizing mentoring display the following characteristics:

- They have a conformist culture in which most critical decisions are made by consensus.

- They have an abundance of hierarchical control in which even routine requests need high levels of approval.

- They are strongly siloed with firmly ingrained internal competition and a lack of cross-functional collaboration.

- They are technologically ridged, with very little personal freedom to access external resources.

Receptive

Organizations that are receptive to modernizing mentoring display the following characteristics:

- They have a creative and imaginative work environment that regularly relies on role-based judgments.
- They have an agile organization with appropriate (role-specific) levels of decision-making autonomy.
- They are highly collaborative, with a free flow of cross-functional cooperation and sharing of internal resources.
- They are technically diverse, allowing personal freedom to access resources on the Internet.

Here is what I learned about creating modern mentoring cultures with organizations. The good news is that most people who make up the organization are ready for modern mentoring. It's those who are in charge who will need to be convinced. However, most organizations are not ideally oriented toward changing their current modes of learning. So, based on these observations, I have a few suggestions that tend to work for organizations that are attempting to modernize mentoring, and answer the question of organizational readiness.

Avoid Starting Too Small

Modern mentoring efforts that start out too small, stay small—and often fail. Traditional mentoring only affects a small hand-selected group of workers. To prove the case for modern mentoring, it is important to show its versatility and range of effectiveness. I encourage you to consider including 10 to 15 percent of the organization in the initial stage of launch, even if your organization is resistant on the readiness continuum. The more receptive your organization measures on the readiness continuum, the more aggressive your initial launch can be.

Fix Something Important

In this book, I have shared how world-leading companies are transforming their learning cultures by leveraging the power of modern mentoring. Every one of them has moved beyond just enhancing a learning process or program to address long-standing business problems. Most organizations have many problems that modern mentoring can address. The more specific and acute the business problem, the more willing organizations will be when it comes to allocating resources and committing to address it. If your organization is more resistant than receptive on the readiness continuum, use modern mentoring to address a critical problem your organization is facing. Your business leaders are not as fascinated with learning methodology as you are. What impresses them is the ability to solve business challenges.

Show Results

It is very important that your modern mentoring efforts create a positive gain for the organization. If you have focused your initiative on solving real business problems instead of just improving current learning processes, then you should be able to show concrete results from your efforts. As I discussed in chapter 3, EMC captured results that showed modern mentoring had positively influenced their employees' final exam scores, proficiency at work, and effectiveness at doing their jobs—on top of saving the company time and money.

These data points are a great example of the tangible proof business leaders need to see before they can be swayed to adopt or change their mentoring programs. Keep in mind that the more resistant your organization is on the readiness continuum, the more evidence you will need of your program's effectiveness.

In that moment, many years ago, while sitting in that auditorium, I realized that I preferred deep thoughts to profound action. I resolved to change that preference and live my life differently—to move beyond romancing deep thoughts to living a life of meaningful action. I broke free of my passive learning orientation and began to create action plans to bring the ideals that I believed in into reality.

That is my challenge to you as you conclude this book. Break free of the things that are holding you back. Push yourself and your organization to expand your ideas, thoughts, methods, and processes. Be an agent of change.

My hope is that you find a way to bring to life through your actions some of the concepts found in this book. The technology exists to support it and your employees are ready to embrace it. So what's stopping you?

Acknowledgments

This book started in earnest as a summation of lessons I've learned during more than 20 years as I've helped my clients construct and manage effective mentoring cultures within their respective organizations. As such, I owe a great debt of gratitude to these clients for their willingness to apply the principles of modern mentoring to real-life business environments. Without them, the ideas I've had swirling in my mind over the years would still be unproven theories.

In that same vein, I knew that a book on modern mentoring would greatly benefit the talent and learning communities, but getting it to the readers was a challenge to overcome. I am very grateful to the team at ATD for their support and expertise in helping me fulfill this dream.

For the past 15 years my personal editor, Laura Francis, has been a partner and teacher who supports me as I get my thoughts into a readable form. Laura has worked with me to refine my voice in the written word and helped me breathe life into such projects as monthly newsletters, articles, instructional copy, marketing materials, and now this book. Thanks for your guidance as I found my voice as a writer.

Chris Graham has been a collaborator and friend for 20 years, in addition to being a remarkable and talented graphic illustrator. Being a visual and conceptual thinker, I am very dependent on graphical representations to fully express my ideas, and Chris is the person I call on to help me accomplish this. Thanks for the beautiful visuals in this book and beyond.

During the last couple of years I have had the pleasure of working with Kristin Boe, who worked with me in the areas of social media marketing and editing (including this book). Kristin has taught me a lot about the Millennial worker, particularly how they consume information and see the world. She has even succeeded in teaching this old Boomer a few new tricks. Thanks for sharing your perspective with me.

Outside my core creative team, there are many who have shaped my understanding of mentoring, with some of the most notable being Tom Reed, Steve Sjogren, Kenneth Henry, Joe Paskowich, Kyle Nabors, Al Buckweitz, Greg Boyer, and Steve Camkin. To each of you, I give heartfelt thanks for the wisdom you shared and the support you have given me.

I have never worked as an independent thought leader, but rather have always been part of a small organization focused on creating world-class mentoring software solutions. It is to the current and former employees of River (formerly known as Triple Creek) that I owe the biggest acknowledgment and thanks. They have sojourned with me through the days when it was very difficult to fulfill the vision of modern mentoring while also serving our clients, who at the time only wanted traditional mentoring. To all of them, I say thank you and job well done on bringing the vision to life.

Finally, I want to thank my family for all the support and patience they have extended to me as I wrote this book—and as I think of new projects to tackle. Your belief in me means more than words can say.

Appendix I

Dispelling Three Myths About Collaborative Learning

Think you know what your employees want when it comes to collaboration and knowledge sharing in the workplace? In a 2013 benchmarking study by Towards Maturity called *New Learning Agenda*, researchers found that:

- 88 percent of learners want to be able to learn at their own pace.
- 77 percent of learners want to engage with online learning.
- Four out of five people are willing to share what they know with others online.
- Seven out of 10 people are motivated by using tools that will help them network and learn from others.
- 86 percent learn what they need to know for work by collaborating with others.

The last statistic should make us all pause. If 86 percent of our employees are learning what they need to know for work by collaborating with others, we must ask ourselves: Are we doing enough to support this practice? Inaccurate assumptions about what workers desire and expect from a learning and collaboration network, the best way to form networks, or why people participate can stymie innovations and adversely affect organizations. Ending these preconceived notions is critical for successful enterprise-wide knowledge sharing and modern mentoring. Here are three myths about collaborative learning networks and how you can combat them.

Myth #1: People only want to connect with like-minded individuals, such as those in their same job function or discipline.

Fact: Today's knowledge workers see the value of expanding their learning networks beyond just those people in their department or location, and they embrace building a diverse network of collaborators from other departments, divisions, functional areas, and locations across the organization. This helps them gain broader insights and access collective knowledge from people who may have a unique perspective on a similar organizational problem.

Myth #2: The greatest knowledge sharing value is gained from connecting with those higher up in the organization.

Fact: This collaboration myth stems from lingering perceptions around the antiquated practice of traditional mentoring. That said, the focus on more expansive modern mentoring and collaborative learning has broadened people's ideas on who they can collaborate with. People use modern mentoring networks to build credibility and experience based on competencies and capabilities, not solely for political posturing or career progression. They seek out people who could use their expertise or who have the information they need, regardless of job title or organizational authority. For example, subordinates can help more senior leaders understand how their decisions affect those below them in the organizational hierarchy. Peers can be a great source of social support and encouragement, since they understand and experience the same organizational pressures, which can lead to breakthrough insight and advice. Superiors can help knowledge seekers understand the big picture, practice foresight, handle more complex issues, and prepare for larger responsibilities.

Myth #3: Knowledge sharing should occur within pre-existing, familiar networks.

Fact: Learning networks function differently than our personal networks (such as LinkedIn or Facebook), which typically expand as we encounter other professionals, but remain largely unchanged when it comes to people exiting or changing roles. The inherent value in an open and inclusive modern mentoring network is that it will morph over time, as individuals' learning needs change and grow. Colleagues with diverse points of view and values will come and go within these networks, they will play different roles at different times, and they will bring with them new connections and new insights as time goes on. Keeping a fresh and ever-changing network of collaborators from throughout the organization will push people to look beyond what they already know so they can explore the emerging opportunities before them.

As advocates for modern mentoring and collaborative learning, we should encourage and educate people to get outside their own typical work networks when looking for new insights and ideas or when developing new skills and capabilities. For it is in this type of open and collaborative behavior that the greatest potential for deep and meaningful learning lies.

Appendix II

Training Community Moderators at Humana

Health care company Humana helps train employees to be moderators in their Learn @ Clinical Collaborative community. The following is what they provide employees to help set expectations and guidelines.

You have been chosen to support Humana's values of Thriving Together and Inspire Health by serving as a community moderator in the Learn @ Clinical Collaborative community.

As a clinician at Humana, or someone who impacts our clinical strategy, you can have a direct impact on how we learn from each other by participating in this exciting initiative.

Purpose: Encourage conversation about and collaboration around the treatment of chronic conditions to enhance learning in the community.

What is a community moderator? The moderator is someone who is an expert on a specific chronic condition and who will help engage conversation about the topic in the knowledge exchange environment (Humana's social learning environment).

Responsibilities include:

- sharing articles, websites, documents, or questions to encourage engagement
- reading posts, answering questions, or offering feedback to participants
- moderating engagement for accuracy of content posted by other participants
- creating case studies to be posted to the Learn @ CC site about your condition of expertise
- moderating engagement for private health information and medical advice—this is not allowed in the community
- being an awesome role model for other clinicians at Humana!

What is the time commitment? The time commitment is approximately one hour each week. This time will be used to interact with participants and post content, so the time can fluctuate based on your availability. However, the community should be visited at least once every 48 hours to maintain involvement.

Appendix III

Practice Exercise: Building Trust

This practice exercise is intended for people who are active participants in your modern mentoring program. I'm sharing it with you so that you can use it as-is or modify it to suit your needs. I strongly urge you to make a questionnaire of this type available online to your participants so that they can easily access and use it as they meet with their mentoring networks and establish trust with one another.

Directions: To help you start thinking in terms of competence, integrity, and caring, use this practice exercise to help build an open dialogue with the people in your mentoring network. Choose one of these three options as a starting point for building trust within your group.

Option 1: Discuss how the people in your mentoring network or group have been able to share one or two particular competencies with you. Highlight how that has helped you and what you gained from their experience.

Option 2: Describe a time when someone in your mentoring network shared a difficult truth with you or followed up on a promise to take action. Explain how this action helped you gain more trust in them.

Option 3: Draw attention to a time when someone in your mentoring network or group openly and compassionately commiserated with you about something. Describe how this helped you or how it reinforced your trust in them.

Appendix IV

Practice Exercise: Developmental Dialogue Model

This practice exercise is intended for people who are active participants in your modern mentoring program. I'm sharing it with you so that you can use it as-is or modify it to suit your needs.

Directions: As an advisor or as someone looking to lead a mentoring conversation, you can use the Developmental Dialogue Model to help learners identify opportunities for their own growth and learning, and as a framework that allows you to work alongside individuals to help them achieve their goals. In order to effectively apply the Developmental Dialogue Model, consider using the following questions for each phase of the conversation. You are encouraged to use this model to support developmental conversations throughout the lifecycle of your modern mentoring relationship.

Reflect:

- What is your current understanding of…?
- What bothers you most about your present situation?
- How would you describe where you are now on this journey?
- What are your current assumptions about…?
- What have you learned so far about yourself?

Envision:

- If you were the best in the world at this task, skill, or position, what would define your success?
- What is the highest result you can hope for?
- What could you accomplish if you had no limitations or restrictions?
- What organizational goals and business needs align with this outcome?
- Where are you currently as compared with where you want to be when you envision your future?

Explore:

- What have others done in similar circumstances that has worked or not worked? Why?
- How could you get additional information, support, or resources?
- If you did nothing, what would change regardless? What would get worse?
- What else might be possible if you changed a few things under your control?
- What is most important to you or nonnegotiable?

Act:

- How would you describe your specific goal in terms of time and measurable results?

- What are some steps you could take? What should you do first?

- Can you commit to this course of action? Are you comfortable with it?

- What elements are controllable versus uncontrollable? What can you do now that is under your control?

References

Adamsky, D.D. 2013. "The 1983 Nuclear Crisis: Lessons for Deterrence Theory and Practice." *Journal of Strategic Studies* 36(1): 4-41.

Branhan, L. 2005. *The 7 Hidden Reasons Employees Leave: How to Recognize the Subtle Signs and Act Before It's Too Late.* New York: AMACOM.

Brennan, B. 2013. Interview with the author on June 14.

Clinton, R., and P. Stanley. 1992. *Connecting: The Mentoring Relationships You Need To Succeed in Life.* Colorado Springs: NavPress.

Corporate Executive Board. 2008. Sales Executive Council: Introduction to Talent Development. PowerPoint presentation.

Corporate Executive Board. 2014. Driving Breakthrough Performance in the New Work Environment. PowerPoint presentation.

Corporate Leadership Council. 2011. *The Power of Peers: Building Engagement Capital Through Peer Interaction.* Arlington, VA: The Corporate Executive Board Company.

Davidson, J. 2014. Interview with the author on September 24.

Di Stefano, G., F. Gino, G. Pisano, and B. Staats. 2014. "Learning by Thinking: How Reflection Aids Performance." Harvard Business School, Working paper 14-093, March 25.

Dreyfus, H.L., and S.E. Dreyfus. 1986. *Mind Over Machine: The Power of Human Intuition and Expertise in the Age of the Computer.* New York: Free Press.

Duggan, M., and A. Smith. 2013. *Social Media Update 2013*. Pew Research Internet Project, December 30. www.pewinternet.org/2013/12/30/social-media-update-2013.

Egan, M.E. 2011. *Global Diversity and Inclusion: Fostering Innovation Through a Diverse Workforce*. New York: Forbes Insights.

Eichinger, R.W., M.M. Lombardo, and D.B. Workman. 2009. High Potential Talent. PowerPoint presentation. Lominger, Korn Ferry.

Fox, Z. 2013. "Seniors Are Fastest Social Media Adopters in U.S." *Mashable*, August 8. http://mashable.com/2013/08/08/senior-citizens-social-media.

Jaques, E. 2006. *Requisite Organization: A Total System for Effective Managerial Organization and Managerial Leadership for the 21st Century*. 2nd ed. Arlington, VA: Cason Hall & Co. Publishers.

Knowles, M. 1970. *The Modern Practice of Adult Education: Andragogy Versus Pedagogy*. New York: Association Press.

Lechner, C., K. Frankenberger, and S.W. Floyd. 2010. "Task Contingencies in the Curvilinear Relationships Between Intergroup Networks and Initiative Performance." *Academy of Management Journal* 53(4): 865-889.

Lombardo, M., and R. Eichinger. 1996. *The Career Architect Development Planner*. Minneapolis, MN: Lominger Limited.

Luft, J., and H. Ingham. 1955. "The Johari Window, a Graphic Model of Interpersonal Awareness." *Proceedings of the Western Training Laboratory in Group Development*. Los Angeles: UCLA.

McKinsey Global Institute. 2012. *The Social Economy: Unlocking Value and Productivity Through Social Technologies*. New York: McKinsey & Company.

Quantum Workplace. 2014. *2014 Recognition Trends Report*. Omaha, NE: Quantum Workplace.

SHRM (Society for Human Resource Management). 2011. *SHRM Survey Findings: Onboarding Practices*. Alexandria, VA: SHRM. www.shrm.org/research/surveyfindings/articles/pages/onboardingpractices.aspx.

Taleo Research. 2011. *Profitable Talent Management.* San Francisco: Taleo.

The University of British Columbia (UBC News). 2013. "Social Networks Make us Smarter." *UBC News,* November 13. http://news.ubc.ca/2013/11/13/social-networks-make-us-smarter.

Towards Maturity. 2013. *New Learning Agenda—Talent: Technology: Change.* London: Towards Maturity. www.towardsmaturity.org/article/2013/05/07/towards-maturity-2013-benchmark-study.

Towards Maturity. 2014. *The Learner Voice Part 1.* London: Towards Maturity. www.towardsmaturity.org/article/2014/04/09/towards-maturity-learner-voice-part-1.

Towers Watson. 2012. *2012–2013 Talent Management and Rewards Survey.* Washington, D.C.: Towers Watson. www.towerswatson.com/en/Insights/IC-Types/Survey-Research-Results/2012/11/2012-2013-talent-management-and-rewards-survey-us-report.

Triple Creek Associates. 2008. *Web-Based Mentoring's Impact on Retention and Productivity.* Greenwood Village, CO: Triple Creek Associates.

Welch, J., and T. Matisak. 2014. "Leadership Lessons in Leadership With Jack Welch." Session at Skillsoft Perspectives 2014, Las Vegas, NV, April 9.

Index

J

Jaques, Elliott, 133
Johari Window, 113

K

Knowledge gathering, 132
Knowledge sharing, 10, 62, 140,
188–190
Knowledge transfer, 26–27, 62
Knowledge workers, 16
Knowles, Malcolm, 22
Kudos, 103–104

L

Lack of complaints, 17
Land and expand
acquisitions, 66
communities of interest,
59–60
company examples of,
56–57
corporate universities, 73–74
definition of, 55
diversity, 60–61
employee resource groups,
64–65
goal of, 55
high-potential development,
65–66
inclusion, 60–61
mergers, 66

MOOCs, 73–74
onboarding, 66–67
performance management,
68–69
retention of employees,
69–70
sales enablement, 70
succession planning, 71
talent development, 72–73
training, 73–74
Leadership
development programs for,
48
mentoring participation by,
14–15
Learners
active, 46, 177
blocked, 46–47, 176–177
engagement of, through
employee lifecycle, 47–50
mentee versus, 39–40
passive, 46–47, 177–178
types of, 176–178
Learning
blended, 150
collaborative, 29, 39,
187–190
connection-based, 128–129
culture of, 27–28
education-based, 147–149,
159
educational efforts as source
of, 149

experiential, 152–153, 159
exposure-based, 159
formal, 149
holistic, 153–156
leveraging employees for, 150
motivation and, 47
peer-to-peer. *See* Peer-to-peer learning
personalized, 157–158
relationship-centered, 9
schematic diagram of, 46
self-directed, 27–28, 174
social. *See* Social learning
transformative, 125
Learning collaboration, 14
Learning connections, 22
Learning environment, 44–45
Learning networks, 151, 189
Listening
empathy and, 89
to employees, 17–18
Lombardo, Michael, 148
Luft, Joseph, 113
Lunch 'n' learns, 51

M

Managers, 171–173
McKinsey Global Initiative, 27
Mentor(s)
advisor versus, 39–40
historical, 8

matching people with, 11–12
misconceptions about, 10
Mentoring
adaptive approach to, 13
barriers to, 12, 37
exclusionary use of, 10
history of, in business world, 9–10
modern. *See* Modern mentoring
traditional. *See* Traditional mentoring
videos about, 52
Mentoring Moments, 52
Mentoring programs
administrators of, 11
connecting to existing programs, 58
direct reports enrolled into, 171–172
evangelists of, 51
marketing of, 50–51
matching people with mentors, 11–12
publicizing of, 50–51
Mentoring software, 42–43
Mergers, 66
Millennials, 20, 26, 48, 141–143, 169
Modern mentoring
benefits of, 24–29, 172
as broad and flexible, 21–22

building blocks of, 20–24
characteristics of, 19
as diverse, 21
experts at all levels, 16–17
focus of, 18
goal of, 101
guidelines for, 28–31
lack of complaints about, 17
leadership participation in,
14–15
networks for, 189–190
objections to, 13
as open and egalitarian, 20,
45
people benefiting most
from, 15
purpose of, 18–19, 30
results of, 181–182
schematic diagram of, 14
as self-directed and personal,
22–23
senior leadership support
for, 14–15
technology and, 16, 24
terminology used with,
14–15, 38–40
traditional mentoring versus,
14, 19
videos about, 52
as virtual and asynchronous,
23–24
*Modern Practice of Adult Education,
The,* 22

Monsanto, 56, 72
MOOCs, 73–74
Morning Cup of Mentoring, 52
Motivation, 47

N
Numbered levels, 106–107

O
Onboarding, 48, 66–67, 88
Organization
barriers within hierarchy of,
107
knowledge transfer in,
26–27
modern mentoring benefits
for, 168–170
readiness of, 178–182
receptive, 180
resistance by, 179
results of modern mentor-
ing for, 181–182
size of mentoring launch in,
180–181
Outcomes, 94

P
Participants, 166–168
Passive communication style, 114
Passive learners, 46–47, 177–178
Peer(s)

expertise profiling and, 108
positive-focused, 101–104
power of, 100
private rankings used to
build, 106
system for, 102
Results, 181–182
Retention of employees, 24–25,
69–70
Reverse mentoring, 129
River mentoring software, 4–5,
15, 60, 62, 72–74, 103, 106,
127, 129, 139
Roadshows, 51

S

Sales enablement, 70
Self-directed learning, 27–28, 174
*7 Hidden Reasons Employees Leave,
The*, 24
70-20-10 model
benefits of, 158
education, 147–149, 159
experience, 147, 152–153,
159
exposure, 147, 151, 159
schematic diagram of, 147
Sharing of personal knowledge,
82
SHRM. *See* Society for Human
Resource Management
Skill building, 157–158

SMEs. *See* Subject matter experts
Social business networks, 42
Social justice, 17, 29
Social learning
collaborative environments
for, 151
description of, 10, 14–15, 17
opportunities for, 48
software for, 42–43
Social media, 56, 142
Social support, 137–138, 189
Society for Human Resource
Management, 67
Sodexo, 62–64, 71, 164
Software, 4–5, 15, 42–43, 60, 62,
72–74, 103, 106, 127, 129, 139
Stakeholders, 37–38
Stanley, Paul, 7
Structured learning, 45
Subject matter experts, 130
Succession planning, 71
Supervisors, 171–173
Synapse, 72

T

Talent development, 72–73
Technology
email, 43–44
intranet, 41–42
modern mentoring and, 16,
24
social business networks, 42

About the Author

Randy Emelo is president and CEO of River, creators of award-winning modern mentoring and social learning software. He has devoted much his life to helping others learn and develop, and his passion for educating people on how they can professionally advance and grow continues to drive his life today.

With more than 25 years of experience in management, training, and leadership development, Randy has worked with military, profit, and nonprofit organizations both nationally and internationally.

Randy is a prolific author, speaker, and thought leader on topics related to mentoring, collaboration, social learning, and talent development. He has worked with hundreds of clients large and small showing them how to blend formal and informal learning into an interactive, relational, and measurable process with social learning and modern mentoring. He holds a master's degree in organizational design and effectiveness from Fielding Graduate University in Santa Barbara, California.

HOW TO PURCHASE ATD PRESS PUBLICATIONS

ATD Press publications are available worldwide in print and electronic format.

To place an order, please visit our online store: www.td.org/books.

Our publications are also available at select online and brick-and-mortar retailers.

Outside the United States, English-language ATD Press titles may be purchased through the following distributors:

United Kingdom, Continental Europe, the Middle East, North Africa, Central Asia, Australia, New Zealand, and Latin America
Eurospan Group
Phone: 44.1767.604.972
Fax: 44.1767.601.640
Email: eurospan@turpin-distribution.com
Website: www.eurospanbookstore.com

Asia
Cengage Learning Asia Pte. Ltd.
Phone: (65)6410-1200
Email: asia.info@cengage.com
Website: www.cengageasia.com

Nigeria
Paradise Bookshops
Phone: 08033075133
Email: paradisebookshops@gmail.com
Website: www.paradisebookshops.com

South Africa
Knowledge Resources
Phone: +27 (11) 706.6009
Fax: +27 (11) 706.1127
Email: sharon@knowres.co.za
Web: www.kr.co.za

For all other territories, customers may place their orders at the ATD online store: **www.td.org/books**.

0215145.62220